All New COOKBOOK FOR DIABETICS AND THEIR FAMILIES

Foreword by Harriet P. Dustan, M.D.

Professor of Medicine and
Associate Director of General Clinical Research Center
University of Alabama at Birmingham

Developed by the Research Nutritionist of the General Clinical Research Center, School of Medicine, and the Registered Dietitians of the Department of Dietetics, University of Alabama at Birmingham.

Oxmoor House®

Library of Congress Catalog Number: 90-062216
ISBN: 0-8487-1062-2

Manufactured in the United States of America
Twelfth Printing 1995

Editor: Joan Erskine Denman
Assistant Editor: Laura Massey
Editorial Assistant: Leigh Anne Roberts
Designer: Design for Publishing
Illustrator: Nancy Johnson

Photographer: Jim Bathie
Photo Stylist: Kay E. Clarke

Cover: Mustardy Oven-Baked Chicken (page 101),
Fresh Broccoli and Noodles (page 138), Bran Muffins
(page 40), California Coleslaw (page 173).

Backcover: Orange Delight (page 203).

CONTENTS

ACKNOWLEDGMENTS

We gratefully acknowledge the contribution of several people who have helped to make the *All New Cookbook for Diabetics and Their Families* possible. We give special thanks to Mandy Berry, Laura Moore, and Cassandra C. Shepherd, Research Cooks, and Kimberly Garrison Nunn, Diet Technician of the General Clinical Research Center, for the many hours spent preparing and testing all the recipes in the book, and to Elizabeth Ivins, Secretary of the GCRC, for her dedication in typing all of the manuscript.

We want to thank Margaret Palmer, M.S., R.D., Margaret Stewart, R.D., Lynn Epps, M.S., R.D., Lisa Mullins, M.S., R.D., Susan Hommerson, M.S., R.D., and Debra Simerly, M.S., R.D., for their contributions of material for the information section of the book; Linda Harbour, R.D., Assistant Director of Dietetics, for her support and suggestions; and Charlotte Knight Beeker, Department of Dietetics, for her efforts in coordinating the contributions from the Department of Dietetics.

We also appreciate the contributions of "favorite" recipes for modification from the registered dietitians at the University Hospitals and the dietetic interns from the Department of Nutrition Sciences.

To Joan Denman, Editor; Laura Massey, Assistant Editor; and Leigh Anne Roberts, Editorial Assistant, from Oxmoor House, Inc., we express gratitude for the support, advice, and many hours spent preparing the final manuscript.

Also, a very special thank you to our patients with diabetes and their families for their helpful suggestions in preparing this book.

Betty E. Darnell, M.S., R.D.
Director of Nutrition, General Clinical Research Center
Sandra Dillon, M.A., R.D.
Associate Director, Department of Dietetics
University of Alabama at Birmingham

FOREWORD

The food we eat can be a major factor in our health and longevity. Although its importance in these regards is much dependent on our inherited genes, we should all follow good dietary habits and eat wisely because we cannot be sure about those genes. And regardless of our genetic inheritance, we all need to avoid obesity which carries its own dangers.

Specific diseases, such as diabetes, also carry their own dangers, many of which can be lessened by good dietary habits. But most people need some guidelines to help establish those habits and maintain them. This *All New Cookbook for Diabetics and Their Families* was developed for that purpose. Not only does it have good recipes, but, as a real dividend, it has all kinds of helpful hints and specific information important for diabetics. One of the nice things about this book is that it's for the whole family, not just the family member with diabetes.

This is not the first cookbook of this type that the University of Alabama at Birmingham (UAB) has published. The first one was the *Cookbook for Diabetics and Their Families* developed by the registered dietitians of the UAB General Clinical Research Center and the Department of Dietetics of the University of Alabama Hospital. It was so successful for diabetics *and* their families that these dietitians thought that another book—this time *All New*—would provide yet more food choices and thus make healthful food an even more pleasant experience.

Harriet P. Dustan, M.D.
Professor of Medicine and
Associate Director of General Clinical Research Center
University of Alabama at Birmingham

INTRODUCTION

Americans are becoming increasingly aware of the importance of good nutrition as a foundation for good health. Most of us have at least one family member who needs or wants to control the amount and kind of food he or she eats. That person may be "watching cholesterol intake" or trying to "lose a few pounds," or may have a condition or disease, such as diabetes, that requires a carefully controlled diet. With the fast-paced life style that Americans live now, mealtime may be one of the few times families are together. However, a "special diet" need not prevent a family from enjoying meals together, nor require that they eat totally different foods.

Our first book, *Cookbook for Diabetics and Their Families*, was developed at the request of many of our patients with diabetes and their families. They asked for help in planning meals and selecting recipes that the entire family could eat and enjoy.

This *All New Cookbook for Diabetics and Their Families* contains many other requested recipes, including numerous family favorites. These recipes have been modified so that the diabetic can use them, and all the recipes were developed and tested in the General Clinical Research Center at the University of Alabama at Birmingham. In addition to the Exchange value for one serving of each recipe, we have included the calorie count plus the cholesterol, sodium, fiber, protein, fat, and carbohydrate content for one serving of each recipe. This information will be helpful to not only the person with diabetes but also to those who are trying to lower cholesterol, reduce sodium intake, and "watch" calories.

This cookbook also includes the new Exchange Lists formulated by The American Dietetic Association and the American Diabetes Association, and the latest dietary guidelines developed by the American Heart Association in cooperation with the two ADA groups.

Our goal in producing this book is to provide good, nutritious recipes for meals that can be shared and enjoyed by the entire family, including the diabetic.

Betty E. Darnell, M.S., R.D.

Eating Smart

Guidelines for Eating Smart

With every news report we hear, we become more aware of the link between our health and what we eat. The message is clear that what we eat today affects how we feel, how we look, and how we perform—today and tomorrow. This message is not news to diabetics or anyone else following a controlled meal plan for their health. But a controlled diet is not the answer for the average person; the answer is to eat smart. This means eating according to the basics of good nutrition which provide a foundation for good health. The goal of this book is to show you that what's nutritionally good for the diabetic is nutritionally good for you and your family. Nutritious can be delicious. Our recipes prove it!

THE BASICS OF NUTRITION

Scientifically speaking, nutrition is the process of ingestion, digestion, absorption, and metabolism of foods, and it is the nutrients in food that perform the different functions that keep our body operating. The major nutrients are carbohydrates, proteins, fats, vitamins, minerals, and water. Carbohydrates and fats provide energy. Fats also transport certain vitamins throughout the body. Proteins help to build, maintain, and repair cells; make important compounds; and transport blood products. Vitamins and minerals don't provide energy, but they do help the body generate and use energy. Water is a solution and transport medium for other nutrients and waste products. Although not a nutrient, fiber performs important functions in the nutritional process by providing roughage to keep nutrients and wastes moving through the system.

This simplified version of nutrients and their functions in the body is not meant to minimize their importance. The relationship of nutrients to overall health is of major concern to health professionals. And because of this concern, The American Dietetic Association, the American Diabetes Association, and the American Heart Association have joined forces to publish dietary guidelines to promote a healthier American public. We have listed these guidelines with an explanation of the major nutrients. Remember, all eight guidelines are important in building a healthful diet.

RECOMMENDED DIETARY GUIDELINES

1. Calorie intake should be appropriate to reach and maintain a reasonable body weight.

A calorie is a measure of energy provided by a nutrient. One gram of carbohydrate equals 4 calories, one gram of protein equals 4 calories, and one gram of fat equals 9 calories. Note that one gram of fat provides more than twice as many calories as one gram of carbohydrate or protein. That's why foods containing fats are so high in calories. If you consume more calories than you use each day, those extra calories become stored somewhere in the body as body fat.

Reaching a reasonable body weight is not easy, especially when there is a lot of weight to lose. The key is to take in fewer calories than you need to conduct your regular activities or to exert more energy than that provided by the calories you consume. Taking in fewer calories doesn't mean starving yourself. It means eating smart or eating more foods high in fiber and avoiding foods high in fats.

Maintaining a reasonable body weight is also difficult unless you have learned to eat smart. The key here is to balance your calorie intake and your energy output, which is no problem when healthy eating habits become so much a part of your lifestyle that they feel natural.

2. Carbohydrate intake should be about 55%, or slightly more than one-half, of the total daily calorie intake. High fiber, complex carbohydrates should be substituted for low fiber, refined carbohydrates.

Simple carbohydrates, or simple sugars, are called simple because they are quickly and easily digested and are rapidly absorbed by the body.

Simple carbohydrates occur naturally in fruits, milk, certain vegetables, and honey.

Complex carbohydrates, or starches, take longer to digest and absorb; they are found in breads, cereals, legumes, and certain vegetables.

Refined, or processed, carbohydrates are found in sugars and syrups, as well as products containing them, such as cookies, cakes, pies, and candies. These are the carbohydrates to avoid whenever possible.

Most carbohydrates can be broken down into glucose, or blood sugar, which requires insulin in order for the body to process it as energy. Insulin is a hormone produced by the pancreas. In persons with diabetes mellitus, the pancreas does not produce enough insulin to process all the glucose in the system, and the resulting build up of blood sugar can cause a physical reaction. Therefore, diabetics need to limit their intake of simple and complex carbohydrates and avoid refined and processed carbohydrates.

Fiber, or roughage, is the structural component of plant foods that we cannot digest. Fiber itself does not provide any energy, but many foods high in fiber, such as wheat and oat bran, other whole grains, dried beans, fruits, and leafy vegetables, are good sources of other major nutrients. Fiber is singled out for attention in the dietary guidelines because of its several important roles in the body. One of these roles is the feeling of "being full" when a food high in fiber is eaten; this helps prevent overeating and, therefore, obesity. Fiber also provides bulk to keep material moving through the digestive system, and it helps to maintain lower levels of serum cholesterol and glucose by binding cholesterol and delaying absorption of foods.

3. Protein intake should be limited to 20% of total daily calories.

Although proteins supply our body with energy, they usually provide less than one-fifth of the calories in our average diet. As a major nutrient they regulate fluid balance; help carry fats, minerals, drugs, and other products in the blood; make antibodies, enzymes, and hormones; and help build and repair body tissues. Proteins are found in both animal and vegetable foods, which differ in quality according to their amino acid content. Amino acids are the building blocks of proteins, but the essential ones cannot be made by the body in sufficient amounts; they must be obtained from foods. Because they contain all the essential amino acids, animal proteins are classified as "complete." Plant proteins, as found in legumes and grains, are considered incomplete. But if you eat a variety of the plant proteins at the same meal, they will complement each other to provide good quality protein. This is the method by which most vegetarians get "complete" proteins in their diet.

> 4. Total fat intake should be limited to 25% of total daily calories. Saturated fat should be less than 10% of total daily calories. Polyunsaturated fats, and especially monounsaturated fats, should be substituted for saturated fats whenever possible. Total dietary cholesterol intake should be less than 300 milligrams a day.

Fats are the most concentrated source of energy in the diet, supplying more than twice as many calories per gram as do proteins or carbohydrates. Fats account for more than one-third of the total calories in a typical diet. However, current guidelines advise us not to consume more total fat per day than 25% to 30% of our total daily calories. Fat is the major form of stored energy, so if more calories are taken into the body than are used as energy, fat will be stored as excess body fat and may put us at risk for certain diseases.

Although excess body fat can become a problem, fat as a nutrient serves several important functions other than providing energy; fat contains essential fatty acids which are needed for growth and to serve as carriers of the fat-soluble vitamins A, D, E, and K. There are three types of fatty acids: polyunsaturated, monounsaturated, and saturated. Polyunsaturated fatty acids are found in vegetable and fish oils and are usually liquid or soft at room temperature; these help lower cholesterol.

Monounsaturated fatty acids are found specifically in nuts, olives, and avocados. Studies show that monounsaturated fats lower "bad" cholesterol but have little effect on "good" cholesterol. Note that the guidelines advise that we select foods containing monounsaturated and polyunsaturated fats instead of those containing saturated fats whenever possible.

Saturated fats are the fatty acids that we should limit, as the guidelines suggest, to less than 10% of our total daily calories. Primarily found in animal foods, such as butter, cheese, and meat fats, saturated fats are also found in coconut oil, palm oil, shortening, and chocolate.

Cholesterol is a fatty substance also found in animal fats. It is needed to build cells and to make hormones and bile acids. However, the liver makes all the cholesterol that your body needs. Eating too much food rich in cholesterol or too much saturated fat creates an excess of cholesterol in your system which is another risk factor for heart disease. Foods high in dietary cholesterol are usually the same animal foods that contain saturated fats. Eggs are notable exceptions; the yolk is very high in cholesterol, but the egg as a whole contains very little saturated fat.

5. Alternative sweeteners may be used in the diet management of people with diabetes mellitus and people with weight problems.

Sugar substitutes do not have the same properties as sucrose (table sugar) but do give foods a sweet taste. Although some substitutes contain calories, in most cases they are used in such small quantities that they do not add much to total caloric intake.

6. Sodium intake should be limited to 3 grams a day.

The increased emphasis on reducing the mineral sodium in the diet was one of the reasons for the 1986 revision of the Exchange Lists. A high intake of sodium has been associated with high blood pressure. Americans now consume as much as 4 to 6 grams of sodium a day, whereas the healthy body can function quite normally on 1/10 teaspoon of salt daily which contains less than 0.2 grams of sodium.

7. Alcohol should be consumed only in moderation.

Nutritionally, alcohol contributes nothing except calories to the body.

8. A wide variety of foods should be consumed.

By eating a variety of foods, you can usually supply your body with all the basic nutrients, including vitamins and minerals. The diet plan based on the Exchange Lists which has been prepared for the diabetic in your family allows for this variety. It provides the diabetic with a measured number of food choices within each food group. By using the Exchange Lists much the same way, you can plan the same well-balanced variety of nutritious meals for your whole family. As a daily guide, serve at least 4 choices from the Starch/Bread group, 5 Meat or Meat substitute choices,

2 Vegetable choices, 2 Fruit choices, 2 Skim Milk choices, and no more than 3 Fat choices. These choices, based on carefully measured amounts, add up to about 1200 calories. Eating for more or fewer calories can be adjusted by varying the amounts of each food choice.

(Note: The diabetic person needs to follow the diet plan as prescribed by the physician or registered dietitian.)

DIET CONTROL FOR YOUR BEST HEALTH

The dietary guidelines are good general principles for everyone to follow in eating to stay well. However, some health conditions require a more controlled diet that is prepared by a physician and strictly followed by the patient. One of these conditions is diabetes mellitus. And because diabetic persons run a greater risk of developing heart disease and atherosclerosis, their diets take into consideration other related conditions, such as obesity, hypertension, and elevated cholesterol.

DIABETES MELLITUS

Diabetes is a condition caused by a lack of available insulin in the body. Insulin is needed to process glucose, a type of simple sugar which is produced when certain foods (particularly those with a carbohydrate content) are digested. If the body doesn't get enough insulin, it cannot process glucose into the heat and energy that the body needs to keep going. If glucose is not processed, it can't be absorbed by the cells and so it collects in the blood causing high levels of blood glucose.

Because diet is a key factor in the treatment of all three types of diabetes, a controlled diet plan for each individual must be prepared by a physician and/or a registered dietitian. Diet plans are designed to be used in conjunction with the Exchange Lists to provide the diabetic persons with a variety of food choices in controlled amounts and at designated times so their food and insulin can be balanced.

Type I diabetes is often called insulin-dependent diabetes. People with Type I diabetes must take daily insulin injections. Their diet is planned so that it works with the injected insulin to help keep blood glucose at an acceptable level. Eating the correct type of food at the appropriate time is important. The diet plan, used along with the Exchange Lists, provides this balanced schedule while allowing variety in the diet.

Type II diabetes is known as non-insulin-dependent diabetes because in many instances a person with Type II can control blood glucose by diet and exercise alone without the use of insulin. Because Type II people are very often overweight, weight loss for them will usually improve blood glucose control.

Some people with Type II diabetes must take pills (oral hypoglycemic agents) and some may even need to have daily insulin injections. With any insulin injections, the timing of meals and snacks is most important.

Gestational diabetes is a form of diabetes which occurs during pregnancy. For some women, diet alone is effective. For others, insulin injections are required. The diet, although similar to the diet for Type I and Type II, allows for the additional nutrient needs of pregnancy. Gestational diabetes usually disappears after pregnancy.

OBESITY

Obesity is a major health problem, particularly for the person with diabetes whose disease has already made it difficult to balance calories and glucose. However, with the help of a physician and/or registered dietitian in designing a meal plan that limits calories, the diabetic can lose weight which in turn will improve glucose control. If you take insulin, you must consult your physician before dieting because insulin doses and diet are so closely related.

Excessive weight for anyone puts that person at risk for the development of certain diseases, one of those being diabetes. But the difficulty of taking off weight and keeping it off is a recognized fact as evidenced by the number of diet books on the market.

This cookbook will prove to be a valuable aid in your effort to lose weight. First of all, the dietary guidelines at the beginning of this book can set the pace for your weight-control program. By taking one guideline a week and incorporating it into your meal planning, you'll be laying the groundwork for a healthier way of eating and for a gradual reduction in weight. The most recent research supports the premise that weight lost gradually is less likely to be regained than weight lost quickly. For most people, a weight loss of 1 to 2 pounds a week is recommended. This reduction can usually be achieved by decreasing your caloric intake 500 to 1000 calories a day.

HYPERTENSION/ELEVATED CHOLESTEROL

Research has shown that proper diet and weight control can have a major impact on decreasing the risk of cardiovascular disease and/or hypertension for most people. Since diabetic persons are at high risk for both these conditions, they should follow a low-fat, low-sodium, low-cholesterol diet based on the dietary guidelines which we have included in this book. Proper diet and weight control sum up what the guidelines are all about.

The 1986 revision of the Exchange Lists by the American Diabetes Association and The American Dietetic Association includes an emphasis on low-fat, low-cholesterol, and low-sodium foods. The recommendations of the American Heart Association to lower fat intake and to control calories are incorporated into the individual diabetic diet. However, people who have hyperlipidemia may need to have their physician and/or dietitian prepare a diet more restricted in fat.

EXERCISE

Regular physical activity can play a key role in the management of most health conditions, including diabetes. Exercise may help decrease insulin requirements, assist in weight control, reduce risk of cardiovascular complications, and improve an overall feeling of well-being. For Type II diabetics, exercise may enhance the body's use of its own insulin.

Also, people with diabetes are usually able to participate in a variety of sports and physical activities. The best exercises for overall health and conditioning are aerobic exercises. These will strengthen heart muscles and enhance the body's capacity to utilize oxygen. Examples of aerobic exercises are walking, jogging, cycling, and swimming. When you are exercising, try to keep a pace that can be sustained for at least 20 minutes with a warm-up before and a cool-down afterwards. At first this pace might be slow, but endurance is built over time. It is the regularity of your exercise that will bring you the most benefits. Start gradually, but keep it up. However, before starting any exercise program, be sure to check with your physician.

ATTITUDE

Often the most difficult part of any diet is the motivation to stick to it. One key to staying motivated is to keep your menus upbeat and interesting. By using the Exchange Lists, your meals can include a large variety of food choices. Take advantage of this variety and be creative! The recipes in this book will help add a little flair and excitement to your diet. Keep in mind the importance of diet for blood glucose control, weight control, and overall good health.

Eating Smart

Meal Planning With Exchanges

The six Exchange Lists, or food groups (listed below), were developed to aid in menu planning for the diabetic. The individual diet plan prescribed by a physician and/or registered dietitian indicates the number of servings from each food group that should be eaten at each meal and snack. All the foods within a group contain approximately the same amount of nutrients and calories per serving, which means that one serving of a food from the starch list may be exchanged (or substituted) for one serving of any other item in the starch list. The chart below shows the amount of nutrients and number of calories in one serving from each food group.

Exchange List	Carbohydrate (grams)	Protein (grams)	Fat (grams)	Calories
Starch/Bread	15	3	trace	80
Meat				
Lean	—	7	3	55
Medium-Fat	—	7	5	75
High-Fat	—	7	8	100
Vegetable	5	2	—	25
Fruit	15	—	—	60
Milk				
Skim	12	8	trace	90
Low-fat	12	8	5	120
Whole	12	8	8	150
Fat	—	—	5	45

In 1986, the American Diabetes Association and The American Dietetic Association revised the Exchange Lists. The fruit list and the starch list now more accurately represent the caloric content of commonly used serving sizes.

EXCHANGE LISTS

STARCH/BREAD LIST

Each item in this list contains approximately 15 grams of carbohydrate, 3 grams of protein, a trace of fat, and 80 calories. Whole grain products average about 2 grams of fiber per serving. Some foods are higher in fiber. Those foods that contain 3 or more grams of fiber per serving are identified with a * symbol.

You can choose your starch exchanges from any of the items on this list. If you want to eat a starch food that is not on this list, the general rule is that:

½ cup of cereal, grain, or pasta is one serving.

1 ounce of a bread product is one serving.

Your dietitian can help you be more exact.

CEREALS, GRAINS, AND PASTA

*Bran cereals, concentrated (such as Bran Buds®, All Bran®)	⅓ cup
*Bran cereals, flaked	½ cup
Bulgur (cooked)	½ cup
Cooked cereals	½ cup
Cornmeal (dry)	2½ tablespoons
Grapenuts	3 tablespoons
Grits (cooked)	½ cup
Other ready-to-eat unsweetened cereals	¾ cup
Pasta (cooked)	½ cup
Puffed cereal	1½ cups
Rice, white or brown (cooked)	⅓ cup
Shredded wheat	½ cup
*Wheat germ	3 tablespoons

* *3 grams or more of fiber per serving*

DRIED BEANS, PEAS, AND LENTILS

*Beans and peas (cooked), such as kidney, white, split, black-eyed	⅓ cup
*Lentils (cooked)	⅓ cup
*Baked beans	¼ cup

STARCHY VEGETABLES

*Corn	½ cup
*Corn on cob, 6 inches long	1 ear
*Lima beans	½ cup
*Peas, green (canned or frozen)	½ cup
*Plantain	½ cup
Potato, baked	1 small (3 ounces)
Potato, mashed	½ cup
Squash, winter (acorn, butternut)	¾ cup
Yam, sweet potato, plain	⅓ cup

BREAD

Bagel	½ (1 ounce)
Bread sticks, crisp, 4 inches long x ½ inch	2 (⅔ ounce)
Croutons, low-fat	1 cup
English muffin	½
Frankfurter or hamburger bun	½ (1 ounce)
Pita, 6 inches across	½
Plain roll, small	1 (1 ounce)
Raisin, unfrosted	1 slice (1 ounce)
*Rye, pumpernickel	1 slice (1 ounce)
Tortilla, 6 inches across	1
White (including French, Italian)	1 slice (1 ounce)
Whole wheat	1 slice (1 ounce)

CRACKERS AND SNACKS

Animal crackers	8
Graham crackers, 2½ inches square	3
Matzoth	¾ ounce
Melba toast	5 slices
Oyster crackers	24
Popcorn (popped, no fat added)	3 cups

Pretzels	¾ ounce
Rye crisp, 2 inches x 3½ inches	4
Saltine-type crackers	6
Whole wheat crackers, no fat added (crisp breads, such as Finn®, Kavli®, Wasa®)	2-4 slices (¾ ounce)

STARCH FOODS PREPARED WITH FAT
(Count as 1 starch/bread serving, plus 1 fat serving.)

Biscuit, 2½ inches across	1
Chow mein noodles	½ cup
Cornbread, 2-inch cube,	1 (2 ounces)
Cracker, round butter type	6
French fried potatoes, 2 inches to 3½ inches long	10 (1½ ounces)
Muffin, plain, small	1
Pancake, 4 inches across	2
Stuffing, bread (prepared)	¼ cup
Taco shell, 6 inches across	2

MEAT LIST

Each serving of meat and substitutes on this list contains about 7 grams of protein. The amount of fat and number of calories varies, depending on what kind of meat or substitute you choose. The meat list is divided into three parts based on the amount of fat and calories: lean meat, medium-fat meat, and high-fat meat. One ounce (one meat exchange) of each includes:

	Carbohydrate (grams)	Protein (grams)	Fat (grams)	Calories
Lean	0	7	3	55
Medium-Fat	0	7	5	75
High-Fat	0	7	8	100

You are encouraged to use more lean and medium-fat meat, poultry, and fish in your meal plan. This will help decrease your fat intake, which may help decrease your risk for heart disease. The items from the high-fat group are high in saturated fat, cholesterol, and calories. You should limit your choices from the high-fat group to three (3) times per week. Meat and substitutes do not contribute any fiber to your meal plan.

Meat and meat substitutes that have 400 milligrams or more of sodium per exchange are indicated with this symbol •

LEAN MEAT AND SUBSTITUTES
(One exchange is equal to any one of the following items.)

Beef:	USDA Good or Choice grades of lean beef, such as round, sirloin, and flank steak; tenderloin; and chipped beef •	1 ounce
Pork:	Lean pork, such as fresh ham; canned, cured, or boiled ham •; Canadian bacon •; tenderloin	1 ounce
Veal:	All cuts are lean except for veal cutlets (ground or cubed). Examples of lean veal are chops and roasts.	1 ounce
Poultry:	Chicken, turkey, Cornish hen (without skin)	1 ounce
Fish:	All fresh and frozen fish	1 ounce
	Crab, lobster, scallops, shrimp, clams (fresh or canned in water •)	2 ounces
	Oysters	6 medium
	Tuna • (canned in water)	¼ cup
	Herring (uncreamed or smoked)	1 ounce
	Sardines (canned)	2 medium
Game:	Venison, rabbit, squirrel	1 ounce
	Pheasant, duck, goose (without skin)	1 ounce
Cheese:	Any cottage cheese	¼ cup
	Grated parmesan	2 tablespoons
	Diet cheeses • (with less than 55 calories per ounce)	1 ounce
Other:	95% fat-free luncheon meat	1 ounce
	Egg whites	3 whites
	Egg substitutes with less than 55 calories per ¼ cup	¼ cup

• *400 milligrams or more of sodium per serving*

MEDIUM-FAT MEAT AND SUBSTITUTES

(One exchange is equal to any one of the following items.)

Beef:	Most beef products fall into this category. Examples are: all ground beef, roast (rib, chuck, rump), steak (cubed, Porterhouse, T-bone), and meatloaf.	1 ounce
Pork:	Most pork products fall into this category. Examples are: chops, loin roast, Boston butt, cutlets.	1 ounce
Lamb:	Most lamb products fall into this category. Examples are: chops, leg, and roast.	1 ounce
Veal:	Cutlet (ground or cubed, unbreaded)	1 ounce
Poultry:	Chicken (with skin), domestic duck or goose (well-drained of fat), ground turkey	1 ounce
Fish:	Tuna • (canned in oil and drained)	¼ cup
	Salmon • (canned)	¼ cup
Cheese:	Skim or part-skim milk cheeses, such as:	
	Ricotta	¼ cup
	Mozzarella	1 ounce
	Diet cheeses • (with 56-80 calories per ounce)	1 ounce
Other:	86% fat-free luncheon meat •	1 ounce
	Egg (high-cholesterol; limit, 3 per week)	1
	Egg substitutes with 56-80 calories per ¼ cup	¼ cup
	Tofu (2½ inches x 2¾ inches x 1 inch)	4 ounces
	Liver, heart, kidney, sweetbreads (high in cholesterol)	1 ounce

HIGH-FAT MEAT AND SUBSTITUTES

Remember, these items are high in saturated fat, cholesterol, and calories, and should be used only three (3) times per week.

(One exchange is equal to any one of the following items.)

Beef:	Most USDA Prime cuts of beef, such as ribs, corned beef •	1 ounce

Pork:	Spareribs, ground pork, pork sausage •	
	(patty or link)	1 ounce
Lamb:	Patties (ground lamb)	1 ounce
Fish:	Any fried fish product	1 ounce
Cheese:	All regular cheeses •, such as	
	American, Blue, Cheddar, Monterey,	
	Swiss	1 ounce
Other:	Luncheon meats •, such as bologna,	
	salami, pimiento loaf	1 ounce
	Sausage •, such as Polish, Italian	1 ounce
	Knockwurst, smoked	1 ounce
	Bratwurst •	1 ounce
	Frankfurter • (turkey or chicken)	1 frank
		(10/pound)
	Peanut butter (contains unsaturated fat)	1 tablespoon

Count as one high-fat meat plus one fat exchange:

	Frankfurter • (beef, pork, or combination)	1 frank
		(10/pound)

VEGETABLE LIST

Each vegetable serving on this list contains about 5 grams of carbohydrate, 2 grams of protein, and 25 calories. Vegetables contain 2-3 grams of dietary fiber. Vegetables which contain 400 milligrams of sodium per serving are identified with a • symbol.

Vegetables are a good source of vitamins and minerals. Fresh and frozen vegetables have more vitamins and less added salt. Rinsing canned vegetables will remove much of the salt.

Unless otherwise noted, the serving size for vegetables (one vegetable exchange) is:

½ cup of cooked vegetables or vegetable juice
1 cup of raw vegetables

Artichoke (½ medium)	Broccoli
Asparagus	Brussels sprouts
Beans (green, wax, Italian)	Cabbage, cooked
Bean sprouts	Carrots
Beets	Cauliflower

• *400 milligrams or more of sodium per serving*

Eggplant
Greens (collard, mustard,
    turnip)
Kohlrabi
Leeks
Mushrooms, cooked
Okra
Onions
Pea pods
Peppers (green)

Rutabaga
Sauerkraut •
Spinach, cooked
Summer squash (crookneck)
Tomato (one large)
Tomato/vegetable juice •
Turnips
Water chestnuts
Zucchini, cooked

Starchy vegetables such as corn, peas, and potatoes are found on the Starch/Bread List. For free vegetables, see Free Foods on page 21.

FRUIT LIST

Each item on this list contains about 15 grams of carbohydrate and 60 calories. Fresh, frozen, and dry fruits have about 2 grams of fiber per serving. Fruits that have 3 or more grams of fiber per serving have a * symbol. Fruit juices contain very little dietary fiber.

The carbohydrate and calorie content for a fruit serving are based on the usual serving of the most commonly eaten fruits. Use fresh fruits or fruits frozen or canned without sugar added. Whole fruit is more filling than fruit juice and may be a better choice for those who are trying to lose weight. Unless otherwise noted, the serving size for one fruit serving is:

½ cup of fresh fruit or fruit juice
¼ cup of dried fruit

FRESH, FROZEN, AND UNSWEETENED CANNED FRUIT

Apple (raw, 2 inches across)	1 apple
Applesauce (unsweetened)	½ cup
Apricots (medium, raw) or	4 apricots
Apricots (canned)	½ cup, or 4 halves
Banana (9 inches long)	½ banana
*Blackberries (raw)	¾ cup
*Blueberries (raw)	¾ cup

• 400 milligrams or more of sodium per serving

Cantaloupe (5 inches across)	⅓ melon
(cubes)	1 cup
Cherries (large, raw)	12 cherries
Cherries (canned)	½ cup
Figs (raw, 2 inches across)	2 figs
Fruit cocktail (canned)	½ cup
Grapefruit (medium)	½ grapefruit
Grapefruit (segments)	¾ cup
Grapes (small)	15 grapes
Honeydew melon (medium)	⅛ melon
(cubes)	1 cup
Kiwi (large)	1 kiwi
Mandarin oranges	¾ cup
Mango (small)	½ mango
*Nectarine (1½ inches across)	1 nectarine
Orange (2½ inches across)	1 orange
Papaya	1 cup
Peach (2¾ inches across)	1 peach, or ¾ cup
Peaches (canned)	½ cup, or 2 halves
Pear	½ large, or 1 small
Pears (canned)	½ cup, or 2 halves
Persimmon (medium, native)	2 persimmons
Pineapple (raw)	¾ cup
Pineapple (canned)	⅓ cup
Plum (raw, 2 inches across)	2 plums
*Pomegranate	½ pomegranate
*Raspberries (raw)	1 cup
*Strawberries (raw, whole)	1¼ cups
Tangerine (2½ inches across)	2 tangerines
Watermelon (cubes)	1¼ cups

DRIED FRUIT

*Apples	4 rings
*Apricots	7 halves
Dates	2½ medium
*Figs	1½
*Prunes	3 medium
Raisins	2 tablespoons

* 3 grams or more of fiber per serving

FRUIT JUICE

Apple juice/cider	½ cup
Cranberry juice cocktail	⅓ cup
Grapefruit juice	½ cup
Grape juice	⅓ cup
Orange juice	½ cup
Pineapple juice	½ cup
Prune juice	⅓ cup

MILK LIST

Each serving of milk or milk products on this list contains about 12 grams of carbohydrate and 8 grams of protein. The amount of fat in milk is measured in percent (%) of butterfat. The calories vary, depending on what kind of milk you choose. The list is divided into three parts based on the amount of fat and calories: skim/very low-fat milk, low-fat milk, and whole milk. One serving (one milk exchange) of each of these includes:

	Carbohydrate (grams)	Protein (grams)	Fat (grams)	Calories
Skim/Very Low-fat	12	8	trace	90
Low-fat	12	8	5	120
Whole	12	8	8	150

Milk is the body's main source of calcium, the mineral needed for growth and repair of bones. Yogurt is also a good source of calcium. Yogurt and many dry or powdered milk products have different amounts of fat. If you have questions about a particular item, read the label to find out the fat and calorie content.

Milk is good to drink, but it can also be added to cereal and to other foods. Many tasty dishes, such as sugar-free pudding, are made with milk. Add life to plain yogurt by adding one of your fruit servings to it.

SKIM AND VERY LOW-FAT MILK

Skim milk	1 cup
½% milk	1 cup
1% milk	1 cup
Low-fat buttermilk	1 cup

Evaporated skim milk	½ cup
Dry nonfat milk	⅓ cup
Plain nonfat yogurt	8 ounces

LOW-FAT MILK

| 2% milk | 1 cup |
| Plain low-fat yogurt (with added nonfat milk solids) | 8 ounces |

WHOLE MILK

The whole milk group has much more fat per serving than the skim and low-fat groups. Whole milk has more than 3¼% butterfat. Try to limit your choices from the whole milk group as much as possible.

Whole milk	1 cup
Evaporated whole milk	½ cup
Whole plain yogurt	8 ounces

FAT LIST

Each serving on the fat list contains about 5 grams of fat and 45 calories.

The foods on the fat list contain mostly fat, although some items may also contain a small amount of protein. All fats are high in calories and should be carefully measured. Everyone should modify fat intake by eating unsaturated fats instead of saturated fats. The sodium content of these foods varies widely. Check the label for sodium information.

UNSATURATED FATS

Avocado	⅛ medium
Margarine	1 teaspoon
★Margarine, diet	1 tablespoon
Mayonnaise	1 teaspoon
★Mayonnaise, reduced-calorie	1 tablespoon
Nuts and Seeds:	
Almonds, dry roasted	6 whole
Cashews, dry roasted	1 tablespoon
Pecans	2 whole
Peanuts	20 small or 10 large

★*If more than one or two servings are eaten, these foods have 400 milligrams or more of sodium.*

Walnuts	2 whole
Other nuts	1 tablespoon
Seeds, pine nuts,	
sunflower (without shells)	1 tablespoon
Pumpkin seeds	2 teaspoons
Oil (corn, cottonseed,	
safflower, soybean,	
sunflower, olive, peanut)	1 teaspoon
★Olives	10 small or
	5 large
Salad dressing, mayonnaise-type	2 teaspoons
mayonnaise-type, reduced-calorie	1 tablespoon
★Salad dressing (all varieties)	1 tablespoon
•reduced-calorie	2 tablespoons

(Two tablespoons of low-calorie salad dressing is a free food.)

SATURATED FATS

Butter	1 teaspoon
★Bacon	1 slice
Chitterlings	½ ounce
Coconut, shredded	2 tablespoons
Coffee whitener, liquid	2 tablespoons
Coffee whitener, powder	4 teaspoons
Cream (light, coffee, table)	2 tablespoons
Cream, sour	2 tablespoons
Cream (heavy, whipping)	1 tablespoon
Cream cheese	1 tablespoon
★Salt pork	¼ ounce

★If more than one or two servings are eaten, these foods have 400 mg. or more of sodium.

FREE FOODS

A free food is any food or drink that contains less than 20 calories per serving. You can eat as much as you want of those items that have no serving size specified. Be sure to spread them out through the day.

Drinks:
Bouillon • or broth
  without fat
Bouillon (low-sodium)
Carbonated drinks,
  sugar-free
Carbonated water
Club soda
Cocoa powder,
  unsweetened
  (1 Tbsp.)
Coffee/Tea
Drink mixes,
  sugar-free
Tonic water,
  sugar-free

Fruit:
Cranberries,
  unsweetened
  (½ cup)
Rhubarb,
  unsweetened
  (½ cup)

Condiments:
Catsup (1 Tbsp.)
Horseradish
Mustard
Pickles •, dill,
  unsweetened
Salad dressing,
  low-calorie
  (2 Tbsp.)
Taco sauce (1 Tbsp.)
Vinegar

Vegetables:
(*raw, 1 cup*)
Cabbage
Celery
Chinese cabbage*
Cucumber
Green onion
Hot peppers
Mushrooms
Radishes
Zucchini*

Salad greens:
Endive
Escarole
Lettuce
Romaine
Spinach

Sweet Substitutes:
Candy, hard, sugar-free
Gelatin, sugar-free
Gum, sugar-free
Jam / Jelly, sugar-free
  (2 tsp.)
Pancake syrup,
  sugar-free
  (1-2 Tbsp.)
Sugar substitutes
  (saccharin,
  aspartame)
Whipped topping
  (2 Tbsp.)

Nonstick pan spray or Vegetable Cooking Spray

Seasonings are also considered free foods and they can be very helpful in making food taste better. However, be careful of how much sodium you use. Read the label, and choose those seasonings that do not contain sodium or salt.

* *3 grams or more of fiber per serving*
• *400 milligrams or more of sodium per serving*

FOOD FOR SICK DAYS

Diabetes may be harder to control during illnesses, such as colds, fever, flu, nausea, and vomiting. Often, these illnesses make it difficult or impossible to eat according to your individualized diet plan. The following guidelines should help in your meal planning for these times. For other special instructions you may need to contact your physician.

1. Continue to take your insulin or hypoglycemic agent as prescribed.
2. Follow your meal plan as closely as possible. Eat only foods and liquids that you can digest easily, such as soups, crackers, cereals, juices, soft drinks, and soft fruits.
3. Try to limit your foods to the starch, fruit, and milk groups. Omit foods from the meat, vegetable, and fat groups during the illness, or until your appetite improves.
4. Drink plenty of liquids, especially if fever, vomiting, or diarrhea is present. If you are following your regular meal pattern, your extra liquids should be non-caloric, such as water, diet soft drinks, or other unsweetened liquids.
5. If you cannot eat solid foods, try sweetened liquids, such as fruit juices, regular soft drinks, popsicles, regular fruit flavored gelatin, and non-carbonated, low-sodium natural thirst quencher, to replace the carbohydrates in regular food. Consume these in only small amounts throughout the day because they are quickly absorbed.
6. Be prepared for an illness by keeping special foods and drinks, such as those recommended above, on hand.
7. If you have problems chewing or swallowing (for example, after dental work), try eating regular foods that have been processed in a blender. Remember to measure foods *before* they are blended.

Below is a list of foods suitable for sick days. Each item can be substituted for 15 grams of carbohydrate or 1 serving of starch or fruit.

Applesauce ½ cup	Cream soups
Apple juice ½ cup	1 cup
Baked custard ½ cup	Broth-based soups
Cooked cereal ½ cup	(such as chicken
Crackers, saltine-type 6	noodle) 2 cups

Carbonated beverages
(containing sugar)
¾ cup (6 oz.)

Ginger ale ¾ cup
Gatorade® 1 cup
Grape juice ⅓ cup

Ice cream ½ cup
Sherbet ¼ cup
Jell-O® (regular) ½ cup
Yogurt, plain 1 cup
Popsicle® (3-oz. size) 1
Toast 1 slice

SNACKS

All of us enjoy snacking between meals. However, if you're on a controlled diet, you need to make sure the snack fits into your program. Most people on diabetic diets have snacks already calculated into their diet plans; these calculated snacks consist of appropriate foods in measured amounts which need to be eaten at designated times. Fortunately, these foods also make healthy snacks for other family members.

Some examples of acceptable snacks are:

Popcorn with Parmesan
cheese
Low-fat cheese and crackers

Fresh fruit and cottage
cheese
Cereal and milk

The Snacks chapter in this book includes other snack recipes which you and your family can enjoy. Free foods may be eaten as snacks too, because they contain less than 20 calories per serving. Some of the free foods that make good snack choices are sugar-free gelatin, lettuce salads with low-calorie salad dressing, dill pickles and sugar-free carbonated beverages.

MEALS FROM YOUR KITCHEN

Eating smart really begins at the planning stage, when you're deciding what to buy and how to prepare it. If you're changing your eating habits to provide a healthier diet for you and your family, the planning stage will be difficult at first—new foods, new brands, new tastes, and new methods of preparation. Just remember, gradual changes are best. Start with the dietary guidelines and begin to make changes based on the first guideline. The following suggestions for purchasing and preparing foods will help you make smart changes.

KNOW WHAT'S ON THE LABEL

When shopping for foods, read the labels of the products before making a purchase. Although it is not usually necessary to buy special foods if someone in your family has diabetes, the information found on the label will be helpful to anyone who is concerned about what's in the food they eat.

Some label information is required by law, whereas some information is included voluntarily by the company. One regulation is that the product ingredients be listed in descending order according to amount. If any nutrition claim is made about a product, the following information must be included on the label: serving size; servings per container; calorie content per serving; protein, carbohydrate, and fat content per serving (in grams); and the percentage of United States Recommended Daily Allowances (RDA) of protein, vitamin A, vitamin C, thiamin, riboflavin, niacin, calcium, and iron.

You can use label information in several ways. First, the list of ingredients lets you know exactly what is in the product. And, because the ingredients are listed in descending order according to the amount in the product, you know what you're paying for. For instance, on an oatmeal label the first ingredient, which is found in the largest amount, is rolled oats. This is what you're paying for. However, fruit drinks often contain more water and sugar than fruit juice, making them an expensive purchase because a large percentage of what you're buying is water.

The amount of protein, carbohydrate, and fat in the product can also be helpful in converting the food to the Exchange List. For example, one serving of oatmeal contains: protein, 5 grams; fat, 2 grams; carbohydrate, 17 grams. You can count one serving of this food as a Starch Exchange (15 grams carbohydrate, 3 grams fat).

Lastly, the information provided includes the RDA for essential nutrients. This information can be used to determine whether or not the product includes the nutrients you expect it to have and whether or not the product provides the essential nutrients at a reasonable price.

Ingredients of particular concern to diabetics and others on a special diet are sugars and fats. Beware of foods labeled "dietetic" because they often contain sugars that are not allowed on special diets. "Dietetic" products sometimes contain flour and milk which can also affect blood glucose levels. Avoid these products if they contain any form of sugar. A detailed explanation of what fats to look for is included in the dietary guidelines; sugars to look for on a label are listed below.

SUGAR

While refined sugar is not recommended for individuals with diabetes or those who are weight conscious, its presence is often difficult to detect because it comes in so many forms. All sugars provide carbohydrate which affects blood glucose levels. Many so-called "sugarless" products contain sweeteners such as sorbitol, xylitol, or mannitol which can also affect blood glucose levels. Thus, even when a product is labeled "sugar free," it may not be allowed in unlimited amounts. These sweeteners are relatively expensive, not widely available, and may cause diarrhea with even a low intake.

There are a number of terms which may appear on food labels to indicate that a product contains sugar. Knowing these terms will help you identify the ingredients that need to be calculated into a meal plan. The following list identifies these terms.

SUGAR TERMS

Brown Sugar:	a soft sugar in which crystals are covered by a film of refined dark syrup
Carbohydrate:	a nutrient made up of sugars and starches
Corn Sugar:	a sugar made by the breakdown of cornstarch
Corn Syrup:	a syrup containing several different sugars that is obtained by the partial breakdown of cornstarch
Dextrin:	a sugar formed by the partial breakdown of starch
Dextrose:	another name for sugar
Fructose:	the simple sugar found in fruit, juices, and honey
Galactose:	a simple sugar found in lactose (milk sugar)
Glucose:	a type of simple sugar found in the blood, derived from food, and used by the body for heat and energy
Honey:	a sweet, thick material made in the honey sac of various bees
Invert Sugar:	a combination of sugars found in fruits
Lactose:	the sugar found in milk
Levulose:	another name for fruit sugar
Maltose:	a crystalline sugar formed by the breakdown of starch
Mannitol:	a sugar alcohol

Mannose:	a sugar from manna and the ivory nut
Maple Sugar:	a syrup made by concentrating the sap of the sugar maple
Molasses:	the thick syrup separated from raw sugar in the manufacturing process of sugar
Sorbitol:	a sugar alcohol
Sorghum:	a syrup from the juice of the sorghum grain grown mainly for its sweet juice
Starch:	a powdery complex chain of sugars; for example, cornstarch
Sucrose:	another name for table sugar
Sugar:	a carbohydrate, including the monosaccharides: fructose, galactose, and glucose—and the disaccharides: sucrose, maltose, and lactose
Xylose:	a wood sugar found in corn cobs, straw, bran woodgum, the bran of seeds, cherries, pears, peaches, and plums
Xylotol:	a sugar alcohol

SUGAR SUBSTITUTES

Many sugar substitutes have been developed for use as a sweetening agent for diabetics and the weight conscious. Recipes in this cookbook were modified to include the use of sugar substitutes.

Sugar substitutes do not have the same properties as sucrose (table sugar) but do give foods a sweet taste; in fact, they are intensely sweet. Although some contain calories, in most cases, substitutes are used in such small quantities that they do not significantly contribute to caloric intake. When using sugar substitutes, remember that they do not have the desired properties for browning, lightness, and tenderness in foods. Some sugar substitutes undergo chemical changes when heated, causing a bitter taste in the finished product.

Various brands and amounts of sugar substitutes should be tested to provide the desired sweetness with minimum bitterness and aftertaste to meet a family's needs. Several brands with recommended substitution equivalents for sugar are listed in the Appendix.

PREPARATION GUIDELINES

Once good, nutritious food has been purchased, make sure your method of preparation will keep that food in its most nutritious state for both special diets and family health. These methods, scattered through-out the recipe section, follow the principles of the diabetic diet and the dietary guidelines which include avoiding sugar and too much fat. These principles can be applied to weight-reduction diets, as well, because sugar provides "empty calories" with no nutrients, and fats contain more than twice the calories of carbohydrates and proteins. Also, the type of fat used in food preparation is important. Animal fats should be avoided because of their high content of saturated fat which increases the choles-terol in the bloodstream.

MEASURING

After properly cooking foods, the next step in preparation is proper measuring. Use your meal plan diet booklet which will tell you what measurement to use for a serving of a particular food. Use the following guidelines in measuring your food.

1. Measure the food as you would eat it—after it is cooked, with any bone, skin, or inedible parts removed.
2. Meats are usually weighed on dietetic scales. Fruits also may be weighed on these scales.
3. Most vegetables, cereals, and fruits can be measured using dry mea-suring cups. If a serving calls for ½ cup, the food should be level with the top of the measuring cup.
4. Liquid measuring cups should be used for fluids, such as milk or fruit juices.
5. Foods such as reduced-calorie margarine, low-calorie mayonnaise substitute, peanut butter without sugar, low-fat sour cream, etc. can be measured using teaspoons or tablespoons. The food should be level and not heaped on the spoon.

Remember, only by measuring will you get the correct amount of calories and carbohydrates in your diet.

SEASONING

Flavor, aroma, and variety can be added to recipes by seasoning foods with herbs and spices instead of fat and salt. When using herbs and spices, start with a small amount. If the taste is too delicate, you can always add more. When using dried rather than fresh herbs, use approxi-mately ¼ teaspoon of the herb for every four servings of food.

Add seasonings to cold foods a few hours before serving to blend flavors. Add seasonings to cooked foods during the last hour of cooking to bring out the best taste and aroma.

Seasoning shakers can be prepared by mixing a blend of several herbs and spices that are either ground or dried, and placing these in a salt or spice shaker. The seasoning shaker may be used to flavor foods during cooking or prior to serving. Two ideas for seasoning shakers follow.

Measure and mix together:

#1	#2
2 teaspoons dry mustard	4 teaspoons onion powder
1 teaspoon thyme	2 teaspoons thyme
1 teaspoon sage	½ teaspoon dry mustard
½ teaspoon marjoram	½ teaspoon curry powder

Be creative; invent your own seasoning shakers.

MEALS AWAY FROM HOME

DINING OUT

For most Americans, "eating out" is no longer a luxury; it is just part of a routine. But for some folks it is a necessity. Approximately one third of the money we spend on food today goes for meals and snacks eaten away from home. And it can be a pleasant experience, even for the diabetic or anyone else on a controlled diet, if foods are selected carefully. The following list suggests some good food choices when eating out.

Appetizers: Clear broth, bouillon, or consommé are "free." Fresh vegetables, such as celery sticks, radishes, cucumbers, and green peppers, may be eaten in moderation. Fresh fruit, soups, juices, shrimp cocktail, chips, and crackers may be eaten but must be counted in your meal plan.

Meat, Poultry, and Fish: Select broiled, baked, roasted, or grilled meats, fish, or poultry. If these items are not on the menu, you may request that an item be specially prepared; some restaurants are willing to make these modifications. Request that gravies and sauces be omitted or served on the side. Avoid casseroles, stews, and fried items, if possible. If a breaded or fried item is selected, count the breading and fat on your meal plan, or remove the breading before eating.

Eggs: Poached, boiled, or scrambled eggs are good choices. Avoid fried eggs or eggs in a cream sauce.

Salads: Select vegetable or fresh fruit salads. Request that the salad dressing be served on the side. You may also use lemon juice or vinegar as a "free" salad dressing. Avoid coleslaw, canned fruit, and gelatin salads. Also, it is best to avoid starchy salads such as pasta salad, potato salad, and three-bean salad.

Breads: Choose plain bread, rolls, toast, muffins, crackers, or bread-sticks; be sure to watch the serving sizes. Remember that some breads, such as biscuits, cornbread, pancakes, and hushpuppies, contain fat and should be counted as a starch and a fat.

Vegetables: Select raw, stewed, steamed, or baked vegetables. Avoid fried vegetables or vegetables in a cream or cheese sauce.

Potatoes: Select baked, steamed, boiled, or mashed potatoes, rice or noodles. Request that margarine and sour cream be served on the side. Avoid fried items or those served in a cream sauce. Check the serving size of baked potatoes when eating out; a potato approximately 2 inches in diameter equals one serving of starch.

Desserts: Fresh fruit or fruit juices are good choices. Occasionally you could choose plain ice cream, sherbet, frozen yogurt, or plain cake, such as sponge or angel food cake. Be sure to watch serving sizes.

FAST FOOD

Fast food restaurants are popular today due to their speed, economy, and convenience. Eating an occasional meal at a fast food restaurant should not compromise your special diet plan if you make wise choices. The choice is important because many of the food items on menus are high in sugar, fat, salt, and calories. However, most fast food restaurants also offer items that will fit into your special diet. Avoid the items that are obviously high in sugar and fat, such as milk shakes, fruit pies, sundaes, and regular soft drinks. Learn the nutritive value of some of your favorite items. Follow your meal plan as closely as possible.

BROWN BAGGING

Brown bag lunches and snacks are often handy (and less expensive) to take to school, to work, on trips, or on picnics. Your meal plan can be adapted to include foods that are easily portable.

When refrigeration is available, a wide variety of items can be carried and stored until mealtime. When no refrigeration is available, avoid foods that spoil quickly, such as meat and egg salads, yogurt, cottage cheese, and puddings and custards containing eggs or milk. A cooler filled with ice will keep foods cold when traveling.

Sandwiches are always popular for brown bag lunches. Use thin-sliced meats and cheeses or leftover meats from home. There are several recipes in this cookbook that may be used for sandwich fillings.

Leftover casseroles, stews, and soups can be packed in a wide-mouth thermos or heated if a microwave oven is available. If refrigeration is available, salads also make convenient portable lunches. Some good choices include low-fat cottage cheese, lettuce or Chef's salads (carry the salad dressing separately), fruit salads, or vegetable salads.

Desserts can also be kept cold in a wide-mouth thermos or kept refrigerated. Other dessert items that do not need refrigeration are fruits, such as apples, oranges, bananas, peaches, plums.

Canned juices, such as tomato or vegetable juices, are easy to pack and can be used as a vegetable exchange. Other ideas for a cold vegetable are raw carrots and celery sticks, a fresh tomato, or homemade coleslaw.

EXPLANATION OF ANALYSIS

The recipes in this cookbook have been nutritionally analyzed for assistance in planning meals that meet nutritional guidelines for diabetics and their families. The analysis for a single serving of each recipe is located in a grid below each recipe title and yield. The analysis states the size of that single serving relative to the recipe's overall yield. A breakdown of nutrients as well as exchanges and calories per serving can also be found in the grid. The breakdown lists carbohydrate, protein, fat, and fiber in grams with cholesterol and sodium listed in milligrams.

Nutrient values are generally listed in whole numbers. If a nutrient is analyzed to have a value of 0.5 or more, it is rounded up to a whole number. If it is found to be less than 0.5, then a trace amount of the nutrient is available and will be indicated by the abbreviation "Tr." If a nutrient has no value in a recipe, "0" will be listed. While fiber is not a nutrient, it is included in our analysis because of its function in aiding the digestive process and in lowering blood sugar. Cholesterol is also not a nutrient. It is included in the analysis of each recipe to aid in the management of dietary cholesterol.

Recipes

Beverages

LOW-CALORIE SPICED TEA MIX
YIELD: 72 servings

EACH SERVING Amount: 1 teaspoon		
Exchanges: Free	**Calories:** 1	**Fat:** Tr.
	Carbo: Tr.	**Fiber:** Tr.
Chol: 0 mg	**Protein:** Tr.	**Sodium:** 1 mg

INGREDIENTS:
¼ cup plus 2 tablespoons sugar-free, orange-flavored drink mix

¼ cup sugar-free, lemonade-flavored drink mix

¾ cup sugar-free iced tea mix

1 teaspoon ground cloves

2 tablespoons ground cinnamon

STEPS IN PREPARATION:
1. Combine all ingredients, stirring until blended. Store mixture in an airtight container.
2. For each serving, place 1 teaspoon mix in a cup. Add 1 cup hot water, stirring well. Serve hot.

LEMON-ORANGE TEA
Yield: 6 servings

EACH SERVING Amount: ¾ cup		
Exchanges: Free	**Calories:** 20	**Fat:** Tr.
	Carbo: 5 gm	**Fiber:** Tr.
Chol: 0 mg	**Protein:** Tr.	**Sodium:** 17 mg

INGREDIENTS:
½ cup boiling water

2 regular-size tea bags

Sugar substitute to equal 2 tablespoons sugar

1½ cups cold water

1 cup unsweetened orange juice

2 tablespoons lemon juice

1 (12-ounce) can diet lemon-lime carbonated beverage

STEPS IN PREPARATION:
1. Pour boiling water over tea bags. Cover and let stand 5 minutes. Remove and discard tea bags. Transfer tea mixture to a medium pitcher, and stir in sugar substitute.
2. Add cold water, orange juice, and lemon juice. Cover and refrigerate at least 1 hour.
3. When ready to serve, add lemon-lime beverage to tea mixture, stirring well. Pour over ice in individual glasses.

CITRUS COOLER
Yield: 7 servings

EACH SERVING Amount: 1 cup		
Exchanges: 1 Fruit	**Calories:** 51	**Fat:** Tr.
	Carbo: 13 gm	**Fiber:** Tr.
Chol: 0 mg	**Protein:** Tr.	**Sodium:** 7 mg

INGREDIENTS:
¾ cup boiling water
½ cup fresh mint leaves, coarsely chopped
4 cups unsweetened lemonade
1 cup unsweetened orange juice
1 cup unsweetened pineapple juice
¾ cup unsweetened grapefruit juice
Sugar substitute to equal ½ cup sugar

STEPS IN PREPARATION:
1. Pour boiling water over mint leaves. Cover and let stand 10 to 20 minutes. Strain mixture, discarding mint leaves. Transfer mint-flavored water to a large pitcher.
2. Add lemonade and remaining ingredients to pitcher, stirring until blended.
3. Cover and refrigerate 2 to 3 hours. Pour into individual glasses to serve.

APRICOT FIZZ
Yield: 6 servings

EACH SERVING Amount: 1 cup		
Exchanges: 1 Fruit	**Calories:** 62	**Fat:** Tr.
	Carbo: 15 gm	**Fiber:** 0 gm
Chol: 0 mg	**Protein:** 1 gm	**Sodium:** 16 mg

INGREDIENTS:
3 cups unsweetened apricot juice

3 cups diet ginger ale

1 tablespoon lemon juice

STEPS IN PREPARATION:
1. Chill apricot juice and ginger ale thoroughly.
2. To serve, combine apricot juice, ginger ale, and lemon juice; stir well, and pour into individual glasses.

PINEAPPLE-PEACH FRAPPÉ
Yield: 3 servings

EACH SERVING Amount: 1 cup		
Exchanges: 1 Fruit	**Calories:** 133	**Fat:** 1 gm
1 Skim Milk	**Carbo:** 23 gm	**Fiber:** Tr.
Chol: 6 mg	**Protein:** 7 gm	**Sodium:** 103 mg

INGREDIENTS:
½ cup canned, water-packed pineapple chunks

½ cup unsweetened pineappple juice

2 canned, water-packed peach halves, diced

1 cup plain, unsweetened low-fat yogurt

1 cup skim milk

Sugar substitute to equal 2 tablespoons sugar

STEPS IN PREPARATION:
1. Combine pineapple, juice, and peaches in container of an electric blender or food processor; process until pureed.
2. Add yogurt, milk, and sugar substitute; continue to process until smooth and thickened.
3. Pour into individual glasses, and serve immediately.

STRAWBERRY SHAKE
Yield: 2 servings

EACH SERVING Amount: 1 cup		
Exchanges: 1 Skim Milk	**Calories:** 105	**Fat:** Tr.
	Carbo: 16 gm	**Fiber:** Tr.
Chol: 3 mg	**Protein:** 8 gm	**Sodium:** 170 mg

INGREDIENTS:
1½ cups skim milk
⅓ cup fresh strawberries
2 tablespoons unsweetened
    orange juice

Sugar substitute to equal 2
    tablespoons sugar
½ cup nonfat buttermilk

STEPS IN PREPARATION:
1. Combine skim milk, strawberries, orange juice, and sugar substitute in container of an electric blender or food processor. Process until strawberries are pureed and mixture is frothy.
2. Transfer mixture to a small pitcher. Stir in buttermilk.
3. Pour into individual glasses, and serve immediately.

HELPFUL HINT: Remember to incorporate skim milk or evaporated skim milk in your diet plan instead of whole milk or cream. Also substitute low-fat cottage cheese for regular cottage cheese to save fat calories.

ORANGE-YOGURT SHAKE
Yield: 5 servings

	EACH SERVING Amount: ½ cup	
Exchanges: 1 Fruit	**Calories:** 102	**Fat:** 1 gm
½ Skim Milk	**Carbo:** 19 gm	**Fiber:** Tr.
Chol: 3 mg	**Protein:** 4 gm	**Sodium:** 50 mg

INGREDIENTS:
1 (6-ounce) can
    unsweetened frozen
    orange juice
    concentrate, thawed and
    undiluted

1 cup skim milk
¾ cup plain, unsweetened
    low-fat yogurt

STEPS IN PREPARATION:
1. Combine all ingredients in container of an electric blender or food processor; process until smooth.
2. Pour into individual glasses, and serve immediately.

CHOCOLATE-BANANA SHAKE
Yield: 3 servings

	EACH SERVING Amount: 1 cup	
Exchanges: 1 Skim Milk	**Calories:** 95	**Fat:** Tr.
	Carbo: 17 gm	**Fiber:** Tr.
Chol: 3 mg	**Protein:** 6 gm	**Sodium:** 85 mg

INGREDIENTS:
2 cups skim milk
1 medium banana, sliced

1 teaspoon unsweetened
    cocoa

STEPS IN PREPARATION:
1. Combine all ingredients in container of an electric blender or food processor; process until frothy.
2. Pour into individual glasses, and serve immediately.

Recipes

Breads and Cereals

TROPICAL MUFFINS
Yield: 1 dozen muffins

EACH SERVING Amount: 1 muffin

Exchanges: 1 Starch	**Calories:** 115	**Fat:** 3 gm
1 Fat	**Carbo:** 19 gm	**Fiber:** Tr.
Chol: 23 mg	**Protein:** 2 gm	**Sodium:** 224 mg

INGREDIENTS:

1¾ cups all-purpose flour
Sugar substitute to equal ¾ cup sugar
2 teaspoons baking powder
¼ teaspoon baking soda
½ teaspoon salt
¼ cup unsweetened grated coconut
3 medium-size ripe bananas, mashed
⅓ cup reduced-calorie margarine, melted
1 egg, beaten
1 teaspoon grated orange rind
⅓ cup unsweetened orange juice
Vegetable cooking spray

STEPS IN PREPARATION:

1. Sift together flour, sugar substitute, baking powder, soda, and salt in a large bowl; stir in coconut, and make a well in center of mixture.
2. Combine bananas, margarine, egg, orange rind, and juice; add to dry ingredients, stirring just until dry ingredients are moistened.
3. Spoon batter into muffin pans coated with cooking spray, filling two-thirds full. Bake at 375° for 25 to 30 minutes or until lightly browned.

HELPFUL HINT: Use all-vegetable margarine or oil instead of butter, lard, or solid shortening when baking. Also, remember that any fat added to bread after baking or to cereals after cooking must be calculated into your diet in order to control calories.

APPLE-ALLSPICE MUFFINS

Yield: 1 dozen muffins

EACH SERVING Amount: 1 muffin

Exchanges: 1 Starch	**Calories:** 108	**Fat:** 3 gm
1 Fat	**Carbo:** 16 gm	**Fiber:** Tr.
Chol: 22 mg	**Protein:** 3 gm	**Sodium:** 186 mg

INGREDIENTS:

¼ cup plus 2 tablespoons
    reduced-calorie
    margarine, divided
Brown sugar substitute to
    equal ¾ cup brown
    sugar, divided
1 egg
1¾ cups all-purpose flour,
    divided

2 teaspoons baking powder
½ teaspoon ground allspice
¼ teaspoon salt
¾ cup skim milk
1 cup peeled, finely
    chopped apple
Vegetable cooking spray
½ teaspoon ground allspice

STEPS IN PREPARATION:

1. Cream ¼ cup margarine in a medium bowl; gradually add
   ½ cup brown sugar substitute, beating at medium speed of
   an electric mixer until mixture is light and fluffy. Add egg,
   and mix well.
2. Combine 1½ cups flour, baking powder, ½ teaspoon
   ground allspice, and salt. Add to creamed mixture
   alternately with skim milk, stirring just until moistened. Stir
   in finely chopped apple.
3. Spoon batter into muffin pans coated with cooking spray,
   filling two-thirds full.
4. Combine remaining ¼ cup brown sugar substitute, ¼ cup
   flour, and ½ teaspoon allspice in a small bowl. Cut in
   remaining 2 tablespoons margarine with a pastry blender
   until mixture resembles coarse meal; sprinkle evenly over
   tops of muffins. Bake at 400° for 20 minutes or until lightly
   browned.

BRAN MUFFINS
Yield: 2 dozen muffins

EACH SERVING Amount: 1 muffin		
Exchanges: 1 Starch	**Calories:** 98	**Fat:** 3 gm
1 Fat	**Carbo:** 15 gm	**Fiber:** Tr.
Chol: 26 mg	**Protein:** 3 gm	**Sodium:** 240 mg

INGREDIENTS:
1 cup hot water
1 cup shreds of wheat bran
   cereal
½ cup reduced-calorie
   margarine
Liquid sugar substitute to
   equal 1 cup sugar
2 cups nonfat buttermilk

2 eggs, beaten
2½ cups all-purpose flour
2½ teaspoons baking soda
½ teaspoon salt
2 cups wheat bran flakes
   cereal
Vegetable cooking spray

STEPS IN PREPARATION:
1. Pour hot water over shreds of wheat bran cereal; let stand at room temperature 10 minutes.
2. Cream margarine and sugar substitute in a large bowl. Add buttermilk, eggs, and soaked bran cereal, beating well at medium speed of an electric mixer. Combine flour, soda, and salt; stir into cereal mixture. Fold in wheat bran flakes cereal. Cover and store in refrigerator until ready to bake. (Batter can be stored in refrigerator up to 1 week.)
3. To bake, spoon batter into muffin pans coated with cooking spray, filling two-thirds full. Bake at 400° for 15 minutes or until done.

OATMEAL-BLUEBERRY MUFFINS
Yield: 1 dozen muffins

EACH SERVING Amount: 1 muffin

Exchanges: 1 Starch	Calories: 127	Fat: 5 gm
1 Fat	Carbo: 16 gm	Fiber: Tr.
Chol: 26 mg	Protein: 3 gm	Sodium: 300 mg

INGREDIENTS:

1 cup plus 2 tablespoons all-purpose flour
6 ounces uncooked regular oats
1 tablespoon baking powder
Sugar substitute to equal 2 tablespoons sugar
½ teaspoon salt
1 cup skim milk
1 egg
¼ cup vegetable oil
1 cup fresh blueberries
Vegetable cooking spray
1 teaspoon ground cinnamon

STEPS IN PREPARATION:

1. Combine flour, oats, baking powder, sugar substitute, and salt in a medium bowl; make a well in center of mixture.
2. Combine milk, egg, and oil; add to dry ingredients, stirring just until moistened. Gently fold in blueberries.
3. Spoon batter into muffin pans coated with cooking spray, filling two-thirds full. Sprinkle cinnamon over muffins, and bake at 425° for 20 to 25 minutes or until lightly browned.

EXERCISE BREAK: No need to go overboard on exercise. Regular mild exercise may be all you'll need to keep in shape. In order to maintain fitness and keep to a schedule of regular exercise, be sure you pick an activity you like.

BLUEBERRY LOAF
Yield: 1 loaf (16 slices)

EACH SERVING Amount: 1 slice		
Exchanges: 1 Starch	**Calories:** 85	**Fat:** 2 gm
	Carbo: 15 gm	**Fiber:** 1 gm
Chol: 16 mg	**Protein:** 2 gm	**Sodium:** 191 mg

INGREDIENTS:

1 cup all-purpose flour
¾ cup whole wheat flour
½ cup shreds of wheat bran cereal
Brown sugar substitute to equal ⅓ cup brown sugar
2 teaspoons baking powder

½ teaspoon baking soda
½ teaspoon salt
¾ cup unsweetened orange juice
1 egg
1 tablespoon vegetable oil
1 cup fresh blueberries
Vegetable cooking spray

STEPS IN PREPARATION:

1. Combine flours, cereal, brown sugar substitute, baking powder, soda, and salt in a medium bowl, stirring until well combined. Set aside.
2. Combine orange juice, egg, and oil in a large bowl; beat at medium speed of an electric mixer until well blended. Gradually add flour mixture, stirring just until moistened. Gently fold in blueberries.
3. Spoon batter into an 8½- x 4½- x 3-inch loafpan coated with cooking spray.
4. Bake at 350° for 50 minutes or until a wooden pick inserted in center comes out clean. Cool in pan 10 minutes; remove from pan, and cool completely on a wire rack.

CALORIE CURB: Vegetable cooking spray saves fat calories! Use it instead of margarines or oils to grease baking pans and skillets—you'll save fat calories.

BANANA-APPLE BREAD

Yield: 1 loaf (16 slices)

EACH SERVING Amount: 1 slice

Exchanges: 1 Starch	**Calories:** 105	**Fat:** 4 gm
1 Fat	**Carbo:** 16 gm	**Fiber:** Tr.
Chol: 35 mg	**Protein:** 2 gm	**Sodium:** 211 mg

INGREDIENTS:

½ cup reduced-calorie margarine

Sugar substitute to equal 1 cup plus 2 tablespoons sugar

2 eggs

1¾ cups all-purpose flour

2¾ teaspoons baking powder

3 medium bananas, chopped

1 cup peeled, coarsely chopped apple

Vegetable cooking spray

STEPS IN PREPARATION:

1. Cream margarine in a large bowl; gradually add sugar substitute, beating at medium speed of an electric mixer until light and fluffy. Add eggs, and beat until thick and lemon colored.
2. Combine flour and baking powder; add to creamed mixture, mixing well. Fold in bananas and apple.
3. Spoon batter into an 8½- x 4½- x 3-inch loafpan coated with cooking spray.
4. Bake at 350° for 1 hour and 5 minutes to 1 hour and 10 minutes or until a wooden pick inserted in center comes out clean. Cool in pan 10 minutes; remove from pan, and cool completely on a wire rack.

NUTRIENT NEWS: Guidelines for health are urging a switch from white bread and other highly processed wheat products to more whole-grain breads and cereals in order to increase fiber in the diet.

CHEESE CASSEROLE BREAD
Yield: 1 loaf (12 slices)

EACH SERVING Amount: 1 slice		
Exchanges: 1 Starch	**Calories:** 116	**Fat:** 4 gm
1 Fat	**Carbo:** 16 gm	**Fiber:** 1 gm
Chol: 19 mg	**Protein:** 4 gm	**Sodium:** 283 mg

INGREDIENTS:

1 cup all-purpose flour
1 cup whole wheat flour
1 tablespoon baking powder
1 tablespoon instant minced
    onion
½ teaspoon salt
Sugar substitute to equal 2
    tablespoons sugar
½ teaspoon dried whole
    Italian herb seasoning,
    crushed

⅓ cup skim milk
¼ cup reduced-calorie
    margarine, melted
2 eggs, beaten
Vegetable cooking spray
1 tablespoon grated
    Parmesan cheese

STEPS IN PREPARATION:

1. Combine flours, baking powder, onion, salt, sugar substitute, and Italian herb seasoning in a medium bowl; make a well in center of mixture. Combine milk, margarine, and eggs; add to dry ingredients, stirring just until moistened.
2. Spoon batter into a round 1½-quart casserole dish coated with vegetable cooking spray. Sprinkle grated Parmesan cheese over top.
3. Bake at 400° for 25 to 30 minutes or until a wooden pick inserted in center comes out clean. Let stand 10 minutes; slice and serve warm, or turn out onto a wire rack, and cool completely before slicing.

CARROT BREAD

Yield: 2 loaves (16 slices each)

EACH SERVING Amount: 1 slice

Exchanges: 1 Starch	**Calories:** 77	**Fat:** 2 gm
	Carbo: 11 gm	**Fiber:** Tr.
Chol: 34 mg	**Protein:** 2 gm	**Sodium:** 157 mg

INGREDIENTS:

4 eggs
Sugar substitute to equal 2
   cups sugar
¼ cup vegetable oil
½ to ¾ cup water
3 cups all-purpose flour
2 teaspoons baking powder

1½ teaspoons baking soda
2 teaspoons ground
   cinnamon
¼ teaspoon salt
2 cups shredded carrots
Vegetable cooking spray

STEPS IN PREPARATION:

1. Combine eggs and sugar substitute in a large bowl; beat at medium speed of an electric mixer until mixture thickens. Gradually add oil and water; beat until well combined.
2. Combine flour, baking powder, soda, cinnamon, and salt; gradually add to egg mixture, stirring just until moistened. Fold in carrots.
3. Spoon batter evenly into two 9- x 5- x 3-inch loafpans coated with cooking spray. Bake at 350° for 1 hour or until a wooden pick inserted in center comes out clean.

NUTRIENT NEWS: The foods you eat should not be evaluated strictly on the basis of their calorie content. Most people on a diet or meal plan tend to choose only those foods that are low in calories. The result is often a "low-calorie diet" that is limited in important nutrients. Keep in mind that those foods that provide the greatest nutrient density per calorie, not just the fewest calories, are the best ones for safe, healthy, and permanent weight loss.

QUICK-AND-EASY ROLLS
Yield: 1 dozen rolls

EACH SERVING Amount: 1 roll		
Exchanges: 1 Starch	**Calories:** 90	**Fat:** 2 gm
	Carbo: 16 gm	**Fiber:** Tr.
Chol: 6 mg	**Protein:** 2 gm	**Sodium:** 215 mg

INGREDIENTS:
2 cups self-rising flour
¼ cup plus 2 tablespoons
    low-calorie mayonnaise
    substitute

1 cup nonfat buttermilk
Vegetable cooking spray

STEPS IN PREPARATION:
1. Combine first 3 ingredients, stirring just until moistened. Spoon batter into muffin pans coated with cooking spray.
2. Bake at 375° for 12 to 15 minutes or until lightly browned.

MEXICAN CORNBREAD
Yield: 10 wedges

EACH SERVING Amount: 1 wedge		
Exchanges: 1 Starch	**Calories:** 112	**Fat:** 4 gm
1 Fat	**Carbo:** 15 gm	**Fiber:** Tr.
Chol: 3 mg	**Protein:** 4 gm	**Sodium:** 498 mg

INGREDIENTS:
1 cup self-rising cornmeal
1 cup (4 ounces) shredded
    low-fat process
    American cheese
1 cup whole kernel corn
1 cup skim milk
½ cup chopped onion

1 (4-ounce) jar diced
    pimiento, drained
⅓ cup reduced-calorie
    margarine
2 tablespoons chopped
    jalapeño peppers
½ teaspoon garlic powder
Vegetable cooking spray

STEPS IN PREPARATION:
1. Combine all ingredients, except cooking spray, stirring well. Pour batter into a 10½-inch cast-iron skillet coated with cooking spray.
2. Bake at 350° for 45 minutes or until golden brown. Cut into 10 wedges, and serve warm.

MOM'S KNEADED BISCUIT WEDGES
Yield: 1 dozen wedges

EACH SERVING Amount: 1 wedge		
Exchanges: 1 Starch	**Calories:** 127	**Fat:** 6 gm
1 Fat	**Carbo:** 16 gm	**Fiber:** Tr.
Chol: 1 mg	**Protein:** 3 gm	**Sodium:** 335 mg

INGREDIENTS:
2 cups all-purpose flour
2½ teaspoons baking powder
½ teaspoon baking soda
Sugar substitute to equal 1 tablespoon sugar
¾ cup reduced-calorie margarine
¾ cup nonfat buttermilk

STEPS IN PREPARATION:
1. Combine flour, baking powder, soda, and sugar substitute in a medium bowl, stirring to blend. Cut in margarine with a pastry blender until mixture resembles coarse meal. Add buttermilk, stirring just until dry ingredients are moistened.
2. Turn dough out onto a lightly floured surface, and knead 8 to 10 times.
3. Divide dough into thirds. Gently shape each third into a ball; place 2 inches apart on an ungreased baking sheet. Flatten each ball into a 1-inch-thick circle, and score each into four wedges.
4. Bake at 400° for 10 to 15 minutes or until golden brown. Separate into wedges, and serve warm.

COTTAGE CHEESE PANCAKES

Yield: 4 pancakes

EACH SERVING Amount: 1 pancake		
Exchanges: 1 Lean Meat	Calories: 38	Fat: Tr.
	Carbo: 1 gm	Fiber: 0 gm
Chol: 0 mg	Protein: 7 gm	Sodium: 112 mg

INGREDIENTS:

½ cup low-fat cottage cheese

4 egg whites

1½ teaspoons all-purpose flour

Vegetable cooking spray

STEPS IN PREPARATION:

1. Combine all ingredients, except cooking spray, in container of an electric blender; process until smooth.
2. For each pancake, pour one-fourth of batter onto a hot nonstick skillet coated with cooking spray.
3. Cook over medium heat, turning pancakes when tops are bubbly. Repeat procedure until all batter is used.

EXERCISE BREAK: The key to walking for your health is consistent rhythm. Major muscle groups should be kept in action at least 30 minutes to reap the most benefits. If you haven't been following a regular walking program, start out with a 15- or 20-minute walk if approved by your physician. But don't just amble along—that's not aerobic exercise. Remember to walk at a slow pace for the first few minutes as a warm-up, then speed up until you can feel your heart begin to beat more rapidly and you begin to breathe more deeply. Some physicians recommend a pace of three miles per hour. Others say speed is less important than regularity—such as putting in an hour to an hour and a half of walking three times a week. Either way, your heart will benefit.

GARLIC MONKEY BREAD

Yield: 1 loaf (16 slices)

EACH SERVING Amount: 1 slice

Exchanges: 1 Starch   **Calories:** 77   **Fat:** Tr.
                              Carbo: 15 gm   **Fiber:** Tr.
Chol: 0 mg   **Protein:** 2 gm   **Sodium:** 130 mg

INGREDIENTS:

1 package dry yeast
1 cup warm water (105° to 115°)
3 cups all-purpose flour, divided
1 teaspoon salt
Vegetable cooking spray

1 tablespoon reduced-calorie margarine, melted
1 clove garlic, minced
1 teaspoon dried parsley flakes
⅛ teaspoon pepper

STEPS IN PREPARATION:

1. Dissolve yeast in warm water in a large bowl; let stand 5 minutes.
2. Combine 1½ cups flour and salt; add to yeast mixture, stirring well. Gradually stir in remaining 1½ cups flour to make a stiff dough.
3. Turn dough out onto a lightly floured surface; cover and let rest 10 minutes. Knead 8 to 10 minutes or until smooth and elastic. Place dough in a bowl coated with cooking spray, turning to grease top. Cover and let rise in a warm place (85°), free from drafts, 1 hour or until dough is doubled in bulk.
4. Combine melted margarine, garlic, parsley, and pepper, stirring well. Roll dough into 1½-inch balls, and dip each in margarine mixture. Layer balls of dough in a 10-inch ring mold. Cover and let rise in a warm place (85°), free from drafts, 1 hour or until doubled in bulk. Bake at 375° for 25 to 30 minutes. Cool in pan 5 minutes; invert onto serving platter, and serve warm.

CINNAMON ROLLS
Yield: 2 dozen rolls

EACH SERVING Amount: 1 roll

Exchanges: 1½ Starch	**Calories:** 130	**Fat:** 3 gm
	Carbo: 23 gm	**Fiber:** Tr.
Chol: 24 mg	**Protein:** 4 gm	**Sodium:** 161 mg

INGREDIENTS:

4 cups all-purpose flour, divided
1 package dry yeast
Sugar substitute to equal ⅓ cup sugar
1 cup skim milk
⅓ cup plus 3 tablespoons reduced-calorie margarine, divided

1 teaspoon salt
2 eggs
Vegetable cooking spray
Sugar substitute to equal ½ cup sugar
2 teaspoons ground cinnamon
¾ cup raisins

STEPS IN PREPARATION:

1. Combine 2 cups flour, yeast, and 1¼ teaspoons sugar substitute in a large bowl.
2. Combine milk, ⅓ cup margarine, and salt in a small saucepan; heat until mixture reaches 120° to 130°. Add liquid mixture to flour mixture. Add eggs, and beat at low speed of an electric mixer 30 seconds. Increase speed to high, and beat 3 minutes. Gradually add remaining 2 cups flour, stirring to make a stiff dough.
3. Turn dough out onto a lightly floured surface. Knead until smooth and elastic (about 8 to 10 minutes). Shape dough into a ball, and place in a bowl coated with cooking spray, turning to grease top. Cover and let rise in a warm place (85°), free from drafts, 1 hour or until doubled in bulk.
4. Punch dough down; divide in half. Cover and let rest 10 minutes. Roll one half of dough to a 12- x 8-inch rectangle. Melt remaining 3 tablespoons margarine over low heat; brush half of melted margarine over shaped dough.

---

5. Combine 2 teaspoons sugar substitute and cinnamon, stirring to blend; sprinkle half over shaped dough. Sprinkle with half of raisins.
6. Roll up jellyroll fashion, beginning at long side; press edges and ends together securely. Cut into 12 slices. Arrange slices in a 9-inch round baking pan coated with cooking spray. Repeat process with remaining dough, melted margarine, sugar substitute mixture, and raisins.
7. Cover and let rise in a warm place (85°), free from drafts, 30 minutes or until doubled in bulk. Bake at 375° for 20 to 25 minutes or until golden brown. Cool slightly; remove from pans, and serve warm.

FARINA AND FRUIT
Yield: 3 servings

EACH SERVING Amount: ½ cup		
Exchanges: 1 Starch	**Calories:** 71	**Fat:** 1 gm
	Carbo: 12 gm	**Fiber:** Tr.
Chol: 1 mg	**Protein:** 3 gm	**Sodium:** 112 mg

INGREDIENTS:

1 cup skim milk
2 pitted dates, chopped
⅛ teaspoon salt
2 tablespoons uncooked
farina
¼ teaspoon vanilla extract

1 teaspoon reduced-calorie margarine
Sugar substitute to equal 2 tablespoons sugar
⅛ teaspoon ground cinnamon

STEPS IN PREPARATION:
1. Combine milk, dates, and salt in a small saucepan; bring to a boil. Gradually stir in farina and vanilla. Reduce heat, and simmer, stirring constantly, 2 to 3 minutes or until thickened.
2. Remove from heat; add margarine and sugar substitute, stirring until margarine melts. Spoon mixture into a serving bowl, and sprinkle with cinnamon. Serve hot.

OATMEAL WITH RAISINS AND CINNAMON
Yield: 4 servings

EACH SERVING Amount: ½ cup		
Exchanges: 1 Starch	**Calories:** 93	**Fat:** 1 gm
	Carbo: 18 gm	**Fiber:** Tr.
Chol: 0 mg	**Protein:** 3 gm	**Sodium:** 197 mg

INGREDIENTS:
1½ cups water
¼ teaspoon salt
2 tablespoons raisins

⅔ cup uncooked
   quick-cooking oats
1 teaspoon ground
   cinnamon

STEPS IN PREPARATION:
1. Combine water, salt, and raisins in a small saucepan; bring to a boil.
2. Stir in oats and cinnamon.
3. Reduce heat, and simmer 1 minute or until water is absorbed.
4. Remove from heat, and serve warm.

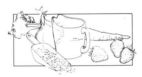

Recipes

Soups

TOMATO BOUILLON
Yield: 4 servings

EACH SERVING Amount: ¾ cup		
Exchanges: 1 Vegetable	Calories: 28	Fat: 1 gm
	Carbo: 5 gm	Fiber: 0 gm
Chol: 0 mg	Protein: 1 gm	Sodium: 253 mg

INGREDIENTS:
1¾ cups water
1½ cups tomato juice
2 teaspoons beef-flavored
    bouillon granules

1 teaspoon Worcestershire
    sauce
⅛ teaspoon hot sauce

STEPS IN PREPARATION:
1. Combine all ingredients in a medium saucepan, stirring until bouillon granules dissolve.
2. Cover and bring to a boil. Reduce heat, and simmer 10 minutes. Serve hot.

FLAVORFUL ONION SOUP
Yield: 4 servings

EACH SERVING Amount: 1½ cups		
Exchanges: 1 Vegetable	Calories: 50	Fat: 3 gm
	Carbo: 5 gm	Fiber: Tr.
Chol: 0 mg	Protein: 0 gm	Sodium: 705 mg

INGREDIENTS:
1 tablespoon
    reduced-calorie
    margarine
1 medium onion, thinly
    sliced
5½ cups water

1 tablespoon plus 2
    teaspoons beef-flavored
    bouillon granules
½ teaspoon Worcestershire
    sauce

STEPS IN PREPARATION:
1. Melt margarine in a large saucepan over low heat; add onion. Cover and cook over low heat 20 minutes or until onion is lightly browned, stirring occasionally.
2. Add water, bouillon granules, and Worcestershire sauce, stirring well.
3. Cover and bring to a boil. Reduce heat, and simmer 10 minutes. Serve hot.

ZUCCHINI SOUP WITH HERBS
Yield: 4 servings

EACH SERVING Amount: 1 cup		
Exchanges: 1 Starch	**Calories:** 94	**Fat:** 2 gm
	Carbo: 18 gm	**Fiber:** 1 gm
Chol: Tr.	**Protein:** 3 gm	**Sodium:** 53 mg

INGREDIENTS:
5 cups chopped zucchini
1 large potato, peeled and cut into 1-inch cubes
1 cup water
3 green onions, thinly sliced
1 tablespoon reduced-calorie margarine, melted

½ cup water
1½ teaspoons dried whole tarragon
½ teaspoon chicken-flavored bouillon granules
½ cup skim milk

STEPS IN PREPARATION:
1. Combine zucchini, potato, and 1 cup water in a small Dutch oven. Cover and bring to a boil. Boil 10 minutes or until crisp-tender (do not drain).
2. Sauté onions in margarine until tender; add to zucchini and potato.
3. Add ½ cup water, tarragon, and bouillon granules, stirring to blend.
4. Add skim milk, and cook over medium heat until thoroughly heated.

BROCCOLI-CAULIFLOWER SOUP
Yield: 15 servings

EACH SERVING Amount: ½ cup

Exchanges: 1 Vegetable	**Calories:** 35	**Fat:** 0 gm
	Carbo: 6 gm	**Fiber:** Tr.
Chol: 1 mg	**Protein:** 3 gm	**Sodium:** 91 mg

INGREDIENTS:

1½ cups water
1 (10-ounce) package frozen chopped broccoli, thawed
1 (10-ounce) package frozen cauliflower, thawed
⅓ cup chopped onion
2 teaspoons chicken-flavored bouillon granules
¼ teaspoon ground mace
1 tablespoon cornstarch
3 cups skim milk, divided
½ teaspoon salt
⅛ teaspoon pepper

STEPS IN PREPARATION:

1. Combine water, broccoli, cauliflower, onion, and bouillon granules in a small Dutch oven. Cover and bring to a boil. Cook 5 to 8 minutes or until vegetables are tender (do not drain). Stir in mace.
2. Process vegetable mixture in batches in container of an electric blender until mixture is smooth.
3. Return mixture to Dutch oven.
4. Dissolve cornstarch in ½ cup milk; stir into vegetable mixture.
5. Add remaining 2½ cups milk, salt, and pepper to vegetable mixture, stirring well.
6. Cook over medium heat, stirring frequently, until mixture is thickened and bubbly.

ENGLISH PEA SOUP
Yield: 8 servings

EACH SERVING Amount: ½ cup

Exchanges: ½ Starch	**Calories:** 46	**Fat:** Tr.
	Carbo: 8 gm	**Fiber:** 1 gm
Chol: Tr.	**Protein:** 3 gm	**Sodium:** 64 mg

INGREDIENTS:

1 (10-ounce) package frozen
    English peas
¼ medium head lettuce
3 ounces fresh spinach
    leaves
½ cup chopped green
    onions

2 teaspoons
    chicken-flavored
    bouillon granules
½ teaspoon dried whole
    chervil, crushed
⅛ teaspoon pepper
1¼ cups water
¾ cup skim milk

STEPS IN PREPARATION:

1. Combine English peas, lettuce, spinach, green onions, bouillon granules, chervil, and pepper in a large saucepan; stir in water.
2. Cover and bring to a boil; reduce heat, and simmer 20 minutes.
3. Process mixture in container of an electric blender or food processor until smooth.
4. Return mixture to saucepan, and stir in milk.
5. Cook over medium heat, stirring frequently, until thoroughly heated.

NUTRIENT NEWS: When it comes to nutrients per calorie, broccoli is a powerhouse. One cup of broccoli is rich in vitamin A, vitamin C, and vitamin B, yet it furnishes only 40 calories. Broccoli is full of calcium and iron, too.

CREAMED POTATO SOUP
Yield: 9 servings

EACH SERVING Amount: ¾ cup

Exchanges: 1 Starch	**Calories:** 85	**Fat:** Tr.
	Carbo: 18 gm	**Fiber:** 1 gm
Chol: Tr.	**Protein:** 3 gm	**Sodium:** 129 mg

INGREDIENTS:
4 medium-size red potatoes, peeled and cut into eighths
1 small onion, peeled and cut into eighths
4 green onions, coarsely chopped
1 clove garlic, minced
2 (10½-ounce) cans no-salt-added chicken broth, undiluted
1 cup skim milk
½ teaspoon salt
⅛ teaspoon white pepper
⅛ teaspoon nutmeg

STEPS IN PREPARATION:
1. Combine potatoes, onion, green onions, garlic, and broth in a heavy 3-quart saucepan.
2. Cover and simmer 20 minutes or until potatoes are tender.
3. Process potato mixture in batches in container of an electric blender or food processor until smooth.
4. Combine pureed mixture with milk and remaining ingredients, stirring until well blended.
5. Reheat soup to serving temperature or cover and refrigerate until thoroughly chilled.

CALORIE CURB: If a soup recipe says to sauté vegetables in butter or oil, steam the vegetables instead, using a small amount of the soup liquid. Or better yet, simply omit this step, and allow the vegetables to cook along with everything else in the soup. Herbs or other fat-free seasonings can be added for flavor, if necessary.

VEGETABLE-CHEESE SOUP
Yield: 6 servings

EACH SERVING Amount: 1 cup

Exchanges: 1 Vegetable	**Calories:** 80	**Fat:** 1 gm
½ Milk	**Carbo:** 12 gm	**Fiber:** 1 gm
Chol: 2 mg	**Protein:** 5 gm	**Sodium:** 310 mg

INGREDIENTS:

1 (10-ounce) package frozen
   mixed vegetables,
   thawed
1 small onion, diced
2 tablespoons all-purpose
   flour
1 teaspoon dried whole
   Italian herb seasoning
¼ teaspoon salt

⅛ teaspoon pepper
1 teaspoon chicken-flavored
   bouillon granules
1 cup water
1 cup skim milk
¼ cup (1 ounce) shredded
   low-fat process
   American cheese
2 teaspoons Dijon mustard

STEPS IN PREPARATION:

1. Combine thawed mixed vegetables and diced onion in a medium saucepan. Combine flour, Italian herb seasoning, salt, and pepper, stirring well; add to vegetables, and stir to coat well.
2. Dissolve bouillon granules in water and milk; add to saucepan, and bring to a boil.
3. Cook, stirring constantly, 5 minutes or until mixture is thickened and bubbly.
4. Reduce heat to low, and add cheese and mustard, stirring to blend. Serve immediately.

GARDEN SOUP
Yield: 10 servings

EACH SERVING Amount: 1 cup		
Exchanges: 1 Starch	**Calories:** 84	**Fat:** 1 gm
	Carbo: 15 gm	**Fiber:** 1 gm
Chol: 6 mg	**Protein:** 4 gm	**Sodium:** 250 mg

INGREDIENTS:

6 cups water
2 cups tomato juice
1 cup diced, peeled potato
1 cup chopped onion
1 cup whole kernel corn
1 cup cooked, drained lima
  beans
¾ cup chopped, cooked
  chicken
½ cup sliced carrots
½ cup chopped celery
2 tablespoons
  chicken-flavored
  bouillon granules
1 teaspoon garlic powder
1½ teaspoons
  Worcestershire sauce

STEPS IN PREPARATION:
1. Combine all ingredients in a large Dutch oven. Cover and bring to a boil.
2. Reduce heat and simmer 45 minutes to 1 hour. Serve hot.

QUICK BEEF SOUP
Yield: 8 servings

EACH SERVING Amount: ½ cup		
Exchanges: 1 Low-fat Meat	**Calories:** 89	**Fat:** 3 gm
½ Starch	**Carbo:** 8 gm	**Fiber:** 1 gm
Chol: 20 mg	**Protein:** 8 gm	**Sodium:** 323 mg

INGREDIENTS:

½ pound lean ground chuck
2 (8-ounce) cans tomato
  sauce
2 cups sliced carrots
¼ cup chopped onion
1 (2½-ounce) jar sliced
  mushrooms
2 cups water

STEPS IN PREPARATION:
1. Cook ground chuck in a large nonstick skillet over medium heat until browned, stirring to crumble. Drain and pat dry with paper towels. Wipe pan drippings from skillet with a paper towel.
2. Return ground chuck to skillet, and add tomato sauce, sliced carrots, chopped onion, and undrained sliced mushrooms. Stir in water.
3. Cover and bring to a boil. Reduce heat, and simmer 30 to 35 minutes or until carrots are tender, stirring occasionally. Serve hot.

NAVY BEAN SOUP
Yield: 11 servings

EACH SERVING Amount: 1 cup		
Exchanges: 2 Starch	**Calories:** 159	**Fat:** 1 gm
	Carbo: 28 gm	**Fiber:** 2 gm
Chol: 0 mg	**Protein:** 9 gm	**Sodium:** 387 mg

INGREDIENTS:
1 (16-ounce) package dried
   navy beans
2 quarts boiling water
1 teaspoon salt
1½ cups diced onion
¼ cup diced celery

1 tablespoon
   reduced-calorie
   margarine, melted
2 cups canned, stewed
   tomatoes

STEPS IN PREPARATION:
1. Soak beans in boiling water in a large Dutch oven 30 minutes. Stir in salt. Cover and bring to a boil. Reduce heat, and simmer 2 hours.
2. Sauté diced onion and celery in melted margarine until tender; add sautéed vegetables and tomatoes to bean mixture, stirring well.
3. Simmer, uncovered, 1 hour or until beans are tender. Serve hot.

COUNTRY CHILI
Yield: 6 servings

EACH SERVING Amount: ⅔ cup		
Exchanges: 1 Starch	**Calories:** 76	**Fat:** 1 gm
	Carbo: 13 gm	**Fiber:** 1 gm
Chol: 0 mg	**Protein:** 3 gm	**Sodium:** 811 mg

INGREDIENTS:
1 large onion, chopped
1 clove garlic, chopped
1 tablespoon reduced-calorie margarine, melted
1 teaspoon salt
1 teaspoon dried whole basil
1 teaspoon chili powder
½ teaspoon dried whole oregano
½ teaspoon dried whole thyme
¼ teaspoon pepper
1 (16-ounce) can whole tomatoes, undrained and chopped
1 (8-ounce) can red kidney beans, undrained

STEPS IN PREPARATION:
1. Sauté onion and garlic in margarine in a large saucepan until tender.
2. Add salt, basil, chili powder, oregano, thyme, and pepper, stirring well.
3. Stir in tomatoes and beans. Simmer, uncovered, 10 to 15 minutes. Serve hot.

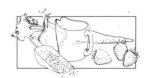

Recipes

Eggs and Cheese

EGG CASSEROLE

Yield: 8 servings

EACH SERVING Amount: ¾ cup		
Exchanges: 1 Starch	**Calories:** 148	**Fat:** 6 gm
1 Medium-fat Meat	**Carbo:** 16 gm	**Fiber:** 1 gm
Chol: 207 mg	**Protein:** 8 gm	**Sodium:** 504 mg

INGREDIENTS:

1½ cups sliced celery
1 cup chopped green pepper
1 medium onion, sliced
1 tablespoon reduced-calorie margarine, melted
1 tablespoon all-purpose flour
1 teaspoon salt
1 (16-ounce) can low-sodium whole tomatoes, undrained

¼ teaspoon hot sauce
6 hard-cooked eggs, chopped
2 cups hot cooked rice (cooked without salt or fat)
Vegetable cooking spray
½ cup (2 ounces) shredded low-fat process American cheese

STEPS IN PREPARATION:

1. Sauté celery, green pepper, and onion in margarine in a 3-quart saucepan until vegetables are tender.
2. Add flour and salt, stirring to blend.
3. Stir in tomatoes and hot sauce; bring to a boil. Reduce heat, and simmer, uncovered, 10 minutes or until mixture is thickened and bubbly, stirring occasionally.
4. Carefully stir in chopped eggs. Spoon rice in bottom of a 2-quart casserole dish coated with cooking spray. Pour egg mixture over rice, and bake, uncovered, at 350° for 25 to 30 minutes or until thoroughly heated. Top with cheese during the last 5 minutes of baking time.

EGGS CREOLE

Yield: 6 servings

EACH SERVING Amount: 1 cup

Exchanges: 1 Skim Milk	**Calories:** 145	**Fat:** 7 gm
1 Fat	**Carbo:** 12 gm	**Fiber:** Tr.
Chol: 264 mg	**Protein:** 8 gm	**Sodium:** 267 mg

INGREDIENTS:

1 tablespoon reduced-calorie margarine
2 teaspoons all-purpose flour
1 cup skim milk
1 cup chopped green pepper
1 cup chopped onion
1 cup undiluted commercial tomato soup
1 teaspoon Worcestershire sauce
6 hard-cooked eggs, coarsely chopped
Vegetable cooking spray
2 tablespoons soft breadcrumbs

STEPS IN PREPARATION:

1. Melt margarine in a small heavy saucepan over low heat; add flour, stirring until smooth. Cook 1 minute, stirring constantly. Gradually add milk; cook over medium heat, stirring constantly, until mixture is thickened and bubbly. Remove from heat, and set aside.
2. Combine pepper and onion in container of electric blender or food processor; process until smooth. Transfer mixture to a medium-size nonstick skillet, and cook over low heat until tender.
3. Add soup and Worcestershire sauce to skillet; continue to cook, uncovered, over low heat until thickened.
4. Layer white sauce, eggs, and soup mixture in a 3-quart casserole dish coated with cooking spray; top with breadcrumbs.
5. Bake at 350° for 20 minutes or until breadcrumbs are browned and mixture is thoroughly heated.

POTATO-MUSHROOM OMELET

Yield: 4 servings

	EACH SERVING Amount: ¼ omelet	
Exchanges: 2 Medium-fat Meat	**Calories:** 177	**Fat:** 7 gm
1 Starch	**Carbo:** 14 gm	**Fiber:** Tr.
Chol: 264 mg	**Protein:** 15 gm	**Sodium:** 376 mg

INGREDIENTS:

1 large baking potato,
   peeled and diced
Vegetable cooking spray
½ cup sliced fresh
   mushrooms
½ cup sliced green onions
4 eggs

4 egg whites
½ cup skim milk
½ teaspoon salt
¼ teaspoon pepper
½ cup (2 ounces) shredded
   low-fat process
   American cheese

STEPS IN PREPARATION:

1. Place diced potato in a small saucepan; add boiling water to cover. Cover and cook 10 minutes. Drain well.
2. Coat a 10-inch skillet with cooking spray; place over medium heat until hot. Sauté parboiled potato 5 minutes. Add mushrooms and onions, and sauté an additional 5 minutes or until vegetables are tender. Spread potato mixture in bottom of a 9-inch square baking dish coated with cooking spray.
3. Combine eggs and egg whites in a large bowl; beat at medium speed of an electric mixer until frothy. Add milk, salt, and pepper, beating until very light and fluffy.
4. Pour egg mixture over potato mixture, and bake at 350° for 20 to 25 minutes or until lightly browned and puffy. Remove from oven, and top with cheese. Serve omelet immediately.

COTTAGE CHEESE OMELET
Yield: 2 servings

EACH SERVING Amount: ½ omelet

Exchanges: 1 Medium-fat Meat	Calories: 67	Fat: 3 gm
	Carbo: 1 gm	Fiber: Tr.
Chol: 132 mg	Protein: 8 gm	Sodium: 603 mg

INGREDIENTS:

1 egg
2 egg whites
1 tablespoon water
1 teaspoon dried parsley
　　flakes
½ teaspoon salt

¼ teaspoon dried whole
　　marjoram
¼ teaspoon pepper
Vegetable cooking spray
1 ounce low-fat cottage
　　cheese

STEPS IN PREPARATION:

1. Combine egg, egg whites, water, and seasonings in a small bowl, stirring well.
2. Coat a medium-size nonstick skillet with cooking spray; place over medium heat until hot enough to sizzle a drop of water. Pour egg mixture into pan.
3. As egg mixture starts to cook, gently lift edges of omelet with a spatula, and tilt pan so that uncooked portion flows underneath.
4. When egg mixture is almost set, spoon cottage cheese over half of omelet; continue cooking until eggs are set.
5. Loosen omelet with a spatula, and fold in half; slide onto serving platter, and serve immediately.

CALORIE CURB: You can reduce the calories as much as 50% in a recipe that calls for ricotta cheese by substituting 1% low-fat or dry-curd cottage cheese. If a smoother texture is desired, cream the cottage cheese in a blender or food processor first.

SPINACH SOUFFLÉ
Yield: 8 servings

EACH SERVING Amount: ½ cup

Exchanges: 1 Vegetable	**Calories:** 77	**Fat:** 4 gm
½ Medium-fat Meat	**Carbo:** 5 gm	**Fiber:** Tr.
Chol: 71 mg	**Protein:** 6 gm	**Sodium:** 306 mg

INGREDIENTS:

Vegetable cooking spray
1 tablespoon grated
  Parmesan cheese
2 tablespoons
  reduced-calorie
  margarine
2 tablespoons all-purpose
  flour
1 cup skim milk
1 teaspoon instant minced
  onion
¼ teaspoon salt

¼ teaspoon hot sauce
⅛ teaspoon ground nutmeg
2 eggs, separated
1 (10-ounce) package frozen
  chopped spinach,
  thawed and well drained
½ cup (2 ounces) shredded
  low-fat process
  American cheese
2 egg whites
¾ teaspoon cream of tartar

STEPS IN PREPARATION:

1. Coat bottom of a 2-quart soufflé dish with cooking spray; dust with Parmesan cheese, and set aside.
2. Melt margarine in a 3-quart saucepan over low heat; add flour, stirring until smooth. Cook 2 minutes, stirring constantly.
3. Gradually add milk, onion, salt, hot sauce, and nutmeg; cook over medium heat, stirring constantly, until thickened and bubbly. Remove from heat.
4. Place egg yolks in a small bowl; beat at medium speed of an electric mixer until thick and lemon colored. Gradually stir one-fourth of hot white sauce into egg yolks; stir mixture into remaining white sauce, adding spinach and shredded cheese. Cook over medium heat 1 minute or until cheese melts.

---

5. Combine 4 egg whites (at room temperature) and cream of tartar; beat until stiff, but not dry. Gently fold into white sauce mixture.
6. Spoon mixture into prepared dish. Bake at 350° for 50 to 60 minutes or until puffed and browned. Serve immediately.

ZUCCHINI QUICHE
Yield: 9 servings

EACH SERVING Amount: 1 wedge		
Exchanges: 1 Medium-fat Meat	**Calories:** 102	**Fat:** 4 gm
1 Vegetable	**Carbo:** 7 gm	**Fiber:** Tr.
Chol: 126 mg	**Protein:** 9 gm	**Sodium:** 278 mg

INGREDIENTS:

1 teaspoon cornstarch
¼ teaspoon dried whole oregano
1 cup canned, stewed tomatoes
1½ cups skim milk
4 eggs
1 tablespoon all-purpose flour
2 cups shredded zucchini

¼ cup chopped onion
½ cup (2 ounces) shredded Swiss cheese
½ cup (2 ounces) shredded low-fat process American cheese
2 tablespoons grated Parmesan cheese
Vegetable cooking spray

STEPS IN PREPARATION:

1. Combine cornstarch and oregano in a small saucepan. Add tomatoes, stirring well; bring to a boil. Reduce heat, and simmer 2 minutes or until thickened. Keep warm.
2. Combine milk, eggs, and flour in a large bowl; beat well, using a wire whisk. Add zucchini, onion, and cheeses, stirring well.
3. Pour egg mixture into a 9-inch round quiche dish coated with cooking spray. Bake at 350° for 1 hour.
4. Spoon tomato mixture over quiche. Cut into wedges, and serve warm.

VEGETARIAN PIZZAS
Yield: 6 servings

EACH SERVING Amount: 1 pizza		
Exchanges: 2 Starch	**Calories:** 194	**Fat:** 3 gm
1 Medium-fat Meat	**Carbo:** 29 gm	**Fiber:** 1 gm
Chol: 9 mg	**Protein:** 13 gm	**Sodium:** 705 mg

INGREDIENTS:
Vegetable cooking spray
½ cup chopped onion
1 clove garlic, minced
4 cups seeded and chopped tomatoes
3 tablespoons red wine vinegar
2 tablespoons minced fresh basil
2 teaspoons dried whole oregano
¼ teaspoon pepper

3 (6-inch) whole wheat pita bread rounds
1 cup (4 ounces) shredded low-fat process American cheese
1 medium-size green pepper, chopped
1 small zucchini, thinly sliced
3 ounces fresh mushrooms, thinly sliced
2 tablespoons grated Parmesan cheese

STEPS IN PREPARATION:
1. Coat a large, heavy skillet with cooking spray; place over medium heat until hot. Add onion and garlic, and sauté until tender.
2. Add chopped tomatoes, vinegar, basil, oregano, and pepper to skillet. Bring to a boil; reduce heat, and simmer, uncovered, 20 minutes or until sauce reduces by one-third, stirring occasionally. Remove tomato mixture from heat, and set aside.
3. Cut a slit around edge of each bread round; carefully split apart. Place split bread rounds on a baking sheet; bake at 450° for 5 minutes or until bread rounds begin to brown. Spread ¼ cup tomato mixture evenly over each toasted round. Sprinkle shredded American cheese equally over each round.

4. Arrange vegetables on top of shredded cheese, and sprinkle with Parmesan cheese.
5. Bake at 450° for 10 minutes or until cheese melts and vegetables are tender.

CHEESY ZUCCHINI WITH TOMATO
Yield: 8 servings

EACH SERVING Amount: ½ cup		
Exchanges: 1 Medium-fat Meat	**Calories:** 116	**Fat:** 5 gm
1 Vegetable	**Carbo:** 6 gm	**Fiber:** 1 gm
Chol: 145 mg	**Protein:** 11 gm	**Sodium:** 539 mg

INGREDIENTS:

Vegetable cooking spray
½ cup chopped onion
1 clove garlic, minced
1 large zucchini, sliced
½ cup (2 ounces) shredded low-fat process American cheese
3 small tomatoes, sliced

4 eggs
½ cup skim milk
¼ teaspoon dried whole oregano
¼ teaspoon dried whole basil
1 tablespoon grated Parmesan cheese

STEPS IN PREPARATION:
1. Coat a small skillet with cooking spray; place over medium heat until hot. Add onion and garlic, and sauté until tender. Remove from heat, and set aside.
2. Layer half of zucchini in a 2-quart shallow baking dish coated with cooking spray. Sprinkle with half each of shredded cheese and sautéed mixture.
3. Repeat layers, with remaining zucchini, shredded cheese, and sautéed mixture. Arrange sliced tomatoes around edge of dish.
4. Combine eggs, milk, and herbs, stirring until blended. Pour evenly over top of vegetables, and sprinkle with Parmesan cheese. Bake, uncovered, at 350° for 40 minutes.

BROCCOLI WITH CHEESE CASSEROLE
Yield: 5 servings

EACH SERVING Amount: 1 cup		
Exchanges: 2 Vegetable	**Calories:** 100	**Fat:** 4 gm
1 Fat	**Carbo:** 10 gm	**Fiber:** 1 gm
Chol: 4 mg	**Protein:** 6 gm	**Sodium:** 791 mg

INGREDIENTS:
1 pound fresh broccoli
1 cup water
½ teaspoon salt
¼ cup chopped onion
¼ cup chopped celery
¼ pound fresh mushrooms, sliced
2 teaspoons reduced-calorie margarine, melted
1 (8-ounce) can sliced water chestnuts, drained
½ cup (2 ounces) shredded low-fat process American cheese, divided
½ (10¾-ounce) can cream of mushroom soup, undiluted
½ cup skim milk
⅛ teaspoon garlic powder
⅛ teaspoon pepper
Vegetable cooking spray

STEPS IN PREPARATION:
1. Trim off large leaves of broccoli; remove tough ends of lower stalks. Wash thoroughly; cut into 1-inch pieces.
2. Bring water to a boil in a large saucepan; add broccoli and salt. Cover, reduce heat, and simmer 5 minutes or until tender. Drain liquid, and set broccoli aside.
3. Sauté onion, celery, and mushrooms in margarine in saucepan until tender. Combine broccoli, sautéed vegetables, and water chestnuts in a large bowl; set aside.
4. Combine ¼ cup cheese, soup, and milk in saucepan; cook over low heat, stirring constantly, until cheese melts. Stir in garlic powder and pepper. Pour over broccoli mixture, tossing lightly to coat.
5. Spoon mixture into a 2-quart casserole coated with cooking spray. Bake at 350° for 25 minutes; sprinkle with remaining ¼ cup cheese. Bake an additional 5 minutes or until cheese melts.

Recipes

Meats

VEAL PARMIGIANA
Yield: 6 servings

EACH SERVING Amount: 1 piece veal cutlet with ⅙ sauce

Exchanges: 3 Lean Meat	**Calories:** 181	**Fat:** 8 gm
1 Vegetable	**Carbo:** 6 gm	**Fiber:** Tr.
Chol: 106 mg	**Protein:** 20 gm	**Sodium:** 628 mg

INGREDIENTS:

1 egg, beaten
½ teaspoon salt
¼ teaspoon pepper
¼ cup soft breadcrumbs
1 tablespoon grated
   Parmesan cheese
1 pound thin veal cutlets,
   cut into 6 serving-size
   pieces

Vegetable cooking spray
1 (8-ounce) can tomato
   sauce
2 (1-ounce) slices part-skim
   mozzarella cheese

STEPS IN PREPARATION:

1. Combine egg, salt, and pepper; beat with a wire whisk until blended. Combine breadcrumbs and Parmesan cheese, stirring well. Dip veal into egg mixture, and dredge in breadcrumb mixture.
2. Sauté veal in a large skillet coated with cooking spray until golden brown.
3. Transfer veal to a shallow baking dish. Pour tomato sauce over veal, and top with cheese slices.
4. Bake at 350° for 15 to 20 minutes. Serve immediately.

CALORIE CURB: Since the exact calorie counts of each cut of beef can vary, check the grade to make sure you're getting the leanest meat. "Prime" and "choice" cuts may be tender and juicy, but they are higher in fat. Purchase leaner cuts that are labeled "good" or "select."

SWISS STEAK
Yield: 6 servings

EACH SERVING Amount: 1 piece steak with ⅙ sauce

Exchanges: 3 Lean Meat	**Calories:** 202	**Fat:** 6 gm
2 Vegetable	**Carbo:** 10 gm	**Fiber:** Tr.
Chol: 72 mg	**Protein:** 25 gm	**Sodium:** 481 mg

INGREDIENTS:

1½ pounds lean round steak, trimmed and cut into 6 serving-size pieces

1 tablespoon reduced-calorie margarine, melted

1 (16-ounce) can stewed tomatoes, undrained

1 small onion, sliced

1 stalk celery, sliced

1 medium carrot, scraped and thinly sliced

1 teaspoon Worcestershire sauce

1 tablespoon all-purpose flour

½ teaspoon salt

¼ cup water

STEPS IN PREPARATION:

1. Place each piece of steak between two sheets of heavy-duty plastic wrap, and flatten to ¼-inch thickness, using a meat mallet or rolling pin.
2. Brown meat on both sides in melted margarine in a large skillet. Drain off excess fat. Add stewed tomatoes, sliced onion, celery, carrot, and Worcestershire sauce to skillet. Cover and cook over low heat 1 hour and 15 minutes or until meat is tender. Transfer meat to a serving platter, and keep warm.
3. Skim excess fat from tomato mixture. Combine flour and salt; add water, and stir until well blended. Stir into tomato mixture. Cook over medium heat, stirring frequently, 2 minutes or until thickened and bubbly.
4. Remove sauce mixture from heat, and pour over meat. Serve immediately.

STIR-FRIED BEEF
Yield: 12 servings

EACH SERVING Amount: ½ cup

Exchanges: 1 Lean Meat	**Calories:** 73	**Fat:** 2 gm
1 Vegetable	**Carbo:** 5 gm	**Fiber:** 1 gm
Chol: 26 mg	**Protein:** 9 gm	**Sodium:** 285 mg

INGREDIENTS:

1 pound lean boneless top round steak, trimmed
⅔ cup water
¼ cup chopped onion
3 tablespoons reduced-sodium soy sauce
1 teaspoon beef-flavored bouillon granules
1 teaspoon Worcestershire sauce
1 clove garlic, minced
½ teaspoon salt
⅛ teaspoon pepper
2 medium carrots, scraped and diagonally sliced
2 cups cauliflower flowerets
Vegetable cooking spray
1 cup sliced fresh mushrooms
1 (6-ounce) package frozen snow pea pods, partially thawed
¼ cup water
1 tablespoon cornstarch

STEPS IN PREPARATION:

1. Partially freeze steak; slice diagonally across grain into ¼-inch strips; set aside.
2. Combine ⅔ cup water, onion, soy sauce, bouillon granules, Worcestershire sauce, garlic, salt, and pepper in a large bowl, stirring well. Add steak, stirring to coat. Cover and refrigerate 1 hour, stirring once. Drain steak, reserving marinade. Set steak aside.
3. Cook carrots and cauliflower in boiling water to cover 3 minutes; drain and set aside.
4. Coat a wok or large skillet with cooking spray; heat at medium high for 2 minutes. Add steak, and stir-fry 3 minutes. Add mushrooms; stir-fry 1 minute. Add pea pods, carrots, and cauliflower; stir-fry 2 minutes or until vegetables are crisp-tender.

---

5. Combine reserved marinade, ¼ cup water, and cornstarch, stirring to blend. Pour over steak mixture, and stir-fry until thickened and bubbly.

Note: Stir-Fried Beef may be served over hot cooked rice that has been cooked without salt or fat. (Check Exchange Lists for value on rice.)

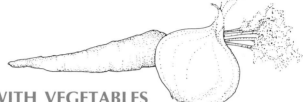

POT ROAST WITH VEGETABLES
Yield: 6 servings

EACH SERVING Amount: 1 slice roast plus ⅙ vegetables		
Exchanges: 2 Lean Meat 1½ Starch	**Calories:** 189 **Carbo:** 21 gm	**Fat:** 4 gm **Fiber:** 1 gm
Chol: 50 mg	**Protein:** 19 gm	**Sodium:** 325 mg

INGREDIENTS:

1 pound lean boneless
   chuck roast, trimmed
Vegetable cooking spray
2 medium onions, peeled
   and sliced
2 stalks celery, sliced
¼ cup water

¼ teaspoon salt
⅛ teaspoon pepper
4 large carrots, scraped and
   sliced
2 medium-size red boiling
   potatoes, peeled and
   coarsely chopped

STEPS IN PREPARATION:
1. Brown boneless chuck roast evenly on all sides over medium heat in a small Dutch oven coated with vegetable cooking spray. Add sliced onion, celery, water, salt, and pepper.
2. Cover Dutch oven, and bake at 350° for 1 hour and 15 minutes. Add sliced carrots and coarsely chopped potatoes; continue to bake, covered, for 1 hour or until meat and vegetables are tender.
3. Transfer roast and vegetables to a serving platter; cut roast into 2-ounce slices. Serve hot.

GINGERED BEEF

Yield: 6 servings

EACH SERVING Amount: ⅔ cup

Exchanges: 2 Lean Meat	**Calories:** 147	**Fat:** 4 gm
1 Starch	**Carbo:** 13 gm	**Fiber:** Tr.
Chol: 49 mg	**Protein:** 17 gm	**Sodium:** 253 mg

INGREDIENTS:

1 cup finely chopped onion
2 cloves garlic, minced
1 teaspoon ground ginger
1 teaspoon ground turmeric
1 teaspoon chili powder
1 pound lean boneless sirloin tip roast, trimmed and cut into ½-inch cubes

Vegetable cooking spray
1 (16-ounce) can whole tomatoes, undrained and chopped
1 cup water
2 teaspoons beef-flavored bouillon granules

STEPS IN PREPARATION:

1. Combine onion, garlic, ginger, turmeric, and chili powder in a medium bowl, stirring well. Add roast, stirring to coat. Cover and refrigerate 2 to 3 hours.
2. Brown roast in a large saucepan coated with cooking spray. Stir in tomatoes, water, and bouillon granules. Bring to a boil; reduce heat, and simmer, partially covered, 1 hour.
3. Uncover and simmer an additional 30 minutes or until meat is tender and liquid is reduced. Serve hot.

Note: Gingered Beef may be served over hot cooked rice that has been cooked without salt or fat. (Check Exchange Lists for value on rice.)

GOULASH WITH GREEN PEPPERS
Yield: 4 servings

EACH SERVING Amount: ¾ cup

Exchanges: 3 Lean Meat	**Calories:** 236	**Fat:** 6 gm
½ Starch	**Carbo:** 7 gm	**Fiber:** 1 gm
Chol: 76 mg	**Protein:** 24 gm	**Sodium:** 84 mg

INGREDIENTS:

1 pound lean boneless
  chuck roast, trimmed
  and cut into 1½-inch
  cubes
Vegetable cooking spray
2 medium onions, chopped

1 cup water
1 tablespoon paprika
1 teaspoon beef-flavored
  bouillon granules
1 small green pepper,
  chopped

STEPS IN PREPARATION:
1. Brown roast over medium heat in a small Dutch oven coated with cooking spray.
2. Add onion, and continue to cook over medium heat 2 to 3 minutes or until onion is tender. Add water, paprika, bouillon granules, and green pepper, stirring well.
3. Cover and cook over low heat 2 hours or until meat is very tender.

Note: Goulash With Green Peppers may be served over hot cooked noodles or rice that has been cooked without salt or fat. (Check Exchange Lists for values on noodles and rice.)

NUTRITION NEWS: "Buy lean" is the watch-word for the health-conscious shopper when purchasing meat in today's market. However, keep in mind that the leanest cuts of meat may contain close to 40% of their calories in fat. Therefore, it's nutritionally smart to keep meat servings small, about 3 ounces, with a whole-grain or vegetable dish as the focus of the meal.

CREOLE MEAT LOAF
Yield (includes sauce): 6 servings

EACH SERVING Amount: 1 slice meat loaf with ⅓ cup sauce

Exchanges: 3 Lean Meat	**Calories:** 160	**Fat:** 7 gm
1 Vegetable	**Carbo:** 7 gm	**Fiber:** Tr.
Chol: 96 mg	**Protein:** 25 gm	**Sodium:** 400 mg

INGREDIENTS:

1 pound lean ground chuck	½ teaspoon dry mustard
½ cup chopped onion	½ teaspoon salt
½ cup skim milk	Vegetable cooking spray
1 egg, beaten	*Creole Sauce (recipe follows)*

STEPS IN PREPARATION:
1. Combine all ingredients, except cooking spray and Creole Sauce, stirring until well combined. Shape into a loaf, and place in an 8½- x 4½- x 3-inch loafpan coated with cooking spray. Bake at 350° for 1 hour. Cool in pan 10 minutes.
2. Invert meat loaf onto serving platter, and pour Creole Sauce over top. Cut meat loaf into 6 slices to serve.

Creole Sauce
Yield (sauce only): 2 cups

EACH SERVING Amount: ⅓ cup

Exchanges: 1 Vegetable	**Calories:** 26	**Fat:** Tr.
	Carbo: 5 gm	**Fiber:** Tr.
Chol: 0 mg	**Protein:** 1 gm	**Sodium:** 161 mg

INGREDIENTS:

Vegetable cooking spray	1½ cups tomato juice
½ cup chopped green pepper	2 tablespoons water
3 tablespoons chopped onion	1 teaspoon cornstarch
¾ cup sliced fresh mushrooms	¼ teaspoon dried whole thyme

STEPS IN PREPARATION:

1. Coat a medium skillet with cooking spray; place over low heat until hot. Add green pepper and onion; sauté 2 to 3 minutes or until tender. Remove from heat, and add mushrooms and tomato juice.
2. Combine remaining ingredients, stirring to blend; add to skillet, and bring to a boil. Boil sauce, stirring constantly, 1 minute or until thickened and bubbly. Serve hot.

ENCHILADA PIE

Yield: 8 servings

EACH SERVING Amount: ½ cup		
Exchanges: 2 Medium-fat Meat	**Calories:** 157	**Fat:** 7 gm
1 Vegetable	**Carbo:** 6 gm	**Fiber:** Tr.
Chol: 44 mg	**Protein:** 16 gm	**Sodium:** 429 mg

INGREDIENTS:

1 pound lean ground chuck
½ cup chopped onion
1 (4-ounce) can tomato
    sauce
1 teaspoon chili powder
½ teaspoon ground cumin
¼ teaspoon salt

¼ teaspoon pepper
4 (6-inch) corn tortillas
¾ cup (3 ounces) shredded
    low-fat process
    American cheese
Vegetable cooking spray
½ cup water

STEPS IN PREPARATION:

1. Cook ground chuck and onion in a large nonstick skillet over medium heat until browned, stirring to crumble. Drain and pat dry with paper towels.
2. Return meat to skillet; stir in tomato sauce and seasonings. Continue to cook over medium heat, stirring constantly, until thoroughly heated.
3. Layer tortillas, meat sauce, and cheese in a 2-quart casserole dish coated with cooking spray; pour water over top. Cover and bake at 400° for 20 minutes. Serve hot.

LASAGNA
Yield: 12 servings

EACH SERVING Amount: 1 portion

Exchanges: 2 Medium-fat Meat   **Calories:** 190   **Fat:** 6 gm
             1 Starch   **Carbo:** 16 gm   **Fiber:** Tr.
Chol: 49 mg   **Protein:** 16 gm   **Sodium:** 393 mg

INGREDIENTS:

1 pound lean ground chuck
1 (16-ounce) can stewed tomatoes, undrained
½ cup water
1 clove garlic, minced
2 teaspoons dried whole Italian herb seasoning
1 (8-ounce) package whole wheat lasagna noodles
1 (10-ounce) package frozen chopped spinach

1 cup low-fat cottage cheese
2 tablespoons grated Parmesan cheese
1 tablespoon dried parsley flakes
1 teaspoon dried whole oregano
Vegetable cooking spray
1 cup (4 ounces) shredded low-fat process American cheese

STEPS IN PREPARATION:

1. Cook ground chuck in a medium skillet over medium heat until browned. Drain and pat dry with paper towels. Wipe skillet with a paper towel.
2. Return meat to skillet, and stir in tomatoes, water, garlic, and Italian herb seasoning. Cover and bring to a boil. Reduce heat, and simmer 20 minutes.
3. Cook noodles according to package directions, omitting salt and fat. Drain well, and set aside.
4. Cook spinach according to package directions, omitting salt and fat. Drain well, and squeeze excess moisture from spinach. Combine spinach and next 4 ingredients, stirring until well combined. Set mixture aside.
5. Place half of cooked noodles in a 12- x 8- x 2-inch baking dish coated with cooking spray. Top with half each of cottage cheese mixture and American cheese. Spread half of meat mixture over top.

---

6. Repeat layers with remaining cooked noodles, cottage cheese mixture, shredded American cheese, and meat mixture. Bake at 350° for 30 minutes. Let stand 10 minutes before serving. Divide into 12 portions, and serve hot.

SIX-LAYER DINNER
Yield: 8 servings

EACH SERVING Amount: ¾ cup		
Exchanges: 1 Starch	**Calories:** 147	**Fat:** 4 gm
1 Medium-fat Meat	**Carbo:** 16 gm	**Fiber:** 1 gm
Chol: 28 mg	**Protein:** 10 gm	**Sodium:** 184 mg

INGREDIENTS:
1 pound lean ground chuck
4 medium-size red boiling potatoes, peeled and cut into ¼-inch slices
2 large carrots, scraped and cut into ¼-inch slices
1 large onion, cut into ¼-inch slices

1 medium-size green pepper, cut into ¼-inch slices
1 (16-ounce) can whole tomatoes, undrained and chopped
¼ teaspoon pepper
⅛ teaspoon dried whole basil

STEPS IN PREPARATION:
1. Cook ground chuck in a large ovenproof skillet with lid over medium heat until meat is browned, stirring to crumble. Drain well, and pat meat dry with paper towels. Wipe skillet with a paper towel.
2. Return ground chuck to skillet, and layer potatoes, carrots, onion, green pepper, and tomatoes over top. Sprinkle with pepper and basil.
3. Cover with ovenproof lid, and bake at 350° for 45 minutes. Serve hot.

GREEN PEPPER CASSEROLE
Yield: 6 servings

EACH SERVING Amount: ⅔ cup		
Exchanges: 1 Medium-fat Meat	**Calories:** 106	**Fat:** 5 gm
1 Vegetable	**Carbo:** 5 gm	**Fiber:** 1 gm
Chol: 71 mg	**Protein:** 10 gm	**Sodium:** 42 mg

INGREDIENTS:

½ pound lean ground chuck
Vegetable cooking spray
3 medium-size green
    peppers, finely chopped
2 medium onions, finely
    chopped
2 tablespoons chopped
    green onions
¼ teaspoon garlic powder

1 egg, beaten
2 tablespoons minced fresh
    parsley
½ teaspoon dried whole
    thyme
¼ teaspoon pepper
⅛ teaspoon ground cloves
⅛ teaspoon ground allspice

STEPS IN PREPARATION:

1. Cook ground chuck in a Dutch oven over medium heat until browned, stirring to crumble. Drain and pat dry with paper towels. Set meat aside. Wipe Dutch oven with a paper towel; coat with cooking spray, and place over low heat until hot.
2. Add green pepper and onions, and sauté 5 minutes or until vegetables are tender. Return meat to Dutch oven with garlic powder. Add egg and next 5 ingredients, stirring until well combined.
3. Spoon mixture into a shallow 2-quart casserole dish coated with cooking spray. Bake at 375° for 20 minutes or until casserole is set.

SWEET-AND-SOUR BEEF AND CABBAGE
Yield: 9 servings

EACH SERVING Amount: 1 cup

Exchanges: 2 Medium-fat Meat	**Calories:** 172	**Fat:** 8 gm
½ Starch	**Carbo:** 9 gm	**Fiber:** 1 gm
Chol: 51 mg	**Protein:** 17 gm	**Sodium:** 265 mg

INGREDIENTS:

1½ pounds lean ground chuck
½ cup chopped onion
½ cup sliced celery
½ cup chopped green pepper
2 tablespoons dried parsley flakes
¾ teaspoon salt

¼ teaspoon garlic powder
1 medium head cabbage, cored and cut into 6 wedges
½ cup tomato sauce
¼ cup vinegar
Brown sugar substitute to equal 3 tablespoons brown sugar

STEPS IN PREPARATION:

1. Cook ground chuck, onion, celery, and green pepper in a large skillet over medium heat until meat is browned and vegetables are tender. Drain and pat dry with paper towels. Wipe skillet with a paper towel. Return meat mixture to skillet, and sprinkle with parsley, salt, and garlic powder. Arrange cabbage over top.
2. Combine tomato sauce, vinegar, and brown sugar substitute, stirring until well blended.
3. Pour sauce mixture over cabbage and meat mixture; cover and bring to a boil. Reduce heat, and simmer 15 to 20 minutes. Serve immediately.

EXERCISE BREAK: "Every little bit counts" could very well apply to exercise. You don't have to run five miles every day. Research shows that even slight increases in physical activity provide beneficial results. Take a walk, mow your lawn, or tend your garden—you'll feel better and sleep better.

SWEET-AND-SOUR PORK

Yield: 10 servings

EACH SERVING Amount: ½ cup

Exchanges: 1 Medium-fat Meat	**Calories:** 97	**Fat:** 3 gm
1 Vegetable	**Carbo:** 6 gm	**Fiber:** Tr.
Chol: 55 mg	**Protein:** 10 gm	**Sodium:** 383 mg

INGREDIENTS:

¼ cup chicken broth

1 egg

1 tablespoon cornstarch

1 tablespoon all-purpose flour

½ teaspoon salt

1 pound lean boneless pork, trimmed and cut into 1-inch cubes

Vegetable cooking spray

1 medium-size green pepper, chopped

½ cup chopped carrot

1 clove garlic, minced

1¼ cups chicken broth

⅓ cup red wine vinegar

2 tablespoons reduced-sodium soy sauce

1 tablespoon cornstarch

¼ cup water

Sugar substitute to equal ¾ cup sugar

STEPS IN PREPARATION:

1. Combine ¼ cup chicken broth, egg, cornstarch, flour, and salt in a medium bowl; beat with a wire whisk until smooth. Dip pork cubes into batter.
2. Coat a large skillet with cooking spray; place over medium heat until hot. Add pork, and cook 5 minutes or until browned. Remove pork; drain on paper towels. Keep warm.
3. Wipe skillet with a paper towel, and coat with cooking spray. Add green pepper, carrot, and garlic; sauté until tender. Stir in 1¼ cups chicken broth, red wine vinegar, and soy sauce.
4. Dissolve cornstarch in water. Stir into vegetable mixture, and bring to a boil. Reduce heat, and simmer, stirring constantly, 1 to 2 minutes or until vegetable mixture is thickened and bubbly.

---

5. Stir in pork cubes and sugar substitute. Cover and simmer until pork is tender, stirring occasionally.

Note: Sweet-and-Sour Pork may be served over hot cooked rice that has been cooked without salt or fat. (Check Exchange Lists for value on rice.)

PORK CHOPS WITH APPLES
Yield: 4 servings

EACH SERVING Amount: 1 chop with ¾ cup apples		
Exchanges: 1½ Starch	**Calories:** 182	**Fat:** 4 gm
1 Medium-fat Meat	**Carbo:** 25 gm	**Fiber:** 1 gm
Chol: 36 mg	**Protein:** 12 gm	**Sodium:** 43 mg

INGREDIENTS:

4 (4-ounce) lean center-cut pork chops, trimmed
1 medium onion, chopped
Vegetable cooking spray
1¼ cups water
1 teaspoon chicken-flavored bouillon granules

¼ teaspoon pepper
3 medium-size cooking apples, peeled and sliced
½ teaspoon ground cinnamon

STEPS IN PREPARATION:

1. Brown pork chops and onion in a large skillet coated with cooking spray.
2. Combine water, bouillon granules, and pepper, stirring to dissolve; add to skillet. Cover and bring to a boil. Reduce heat, and simmer 20 minutes. Skim off fat.
3. Add apple slices and cinnamon to mixture in skillet. Cover and simmer an additional 15 minutes. Transfer to a serving platter, and serve hot.

BAKED HAM WITH PINEAPPLE
Yield: 12 servings

EACH SERVING Amount: 1 slice ham		
Exchanges: 2 Medium-fat Meat	**Calories:** 174	**Fat:** 12 gm
	Carbo: 1 gm	**Fiber:** Tr.
Chol: 35 mg	**Protein:** 14 gm	**Sodium:** 807 mg

INGREDIENTS:
1 (2-pound) fully cooked
    boneless smoked ham
20 whole cloves
4 slices unsweetened
    canned pineapple,
    drained

½ cup diet ginger ale
1 teaspoon ground
    cinnamon

STEPS IN PREPARATION:
1. Remove and discard casing from ham. Score top of ham in a diamond design, and stud with cloves.
2. Place ham in a shallow baking dish, and arrange pineapple slices over top. Pour ginger ale over ham, and evenly sprinkle each pineapple slice with cinnamon.
3. Bake ham at 325° for 25 to 30 minutes or until thoroughly heated. Cut into 12 slices, and serve.

Recipes

Poultry

SPINACH-STUFFED CHICKEN ROLLS
Yield: 8 servings

EACH SERVING Amount: 1 chicken roll

Exchanges: 2 Lean Meat	**Calories:** 105	**Fat:** 1 gm
1 Vegetable	**Carbo:** 6 gm	**Fiber:** 1 gm
Chol: 36 mg	**Protein:** 17 gm	**Sodium:** 327 mg

INGREDIENTS:

1 small onion, chopped

¼ pound fresh mushrooms, chopped

Vegetable cooking spray

1 (10-ounce) package frozen chopped spinach, thawed

2 tablespoons grated Parmesan cheese

1 tablespoon chili sauce

½ teaspoon dried whole basil

½ teaspoon grated lemon rind

¼ teaspoon salt

8 (2-ounce) skinned, boned chicken breast halves

1 (16-ounce) can whole tomatoes, drained and chopped

⅓ cup finely chopped onion

1 clove garlic, crushed

½ teaspoon dried whole Italian herb seasoning

¼ teaspoon pepper

2 tablespoons tomato sauce

STEPS IN PREPARATION:

1. Combine 1 chopped onion and mushrooms in a shallow 2-quart casserole dish coated with cooking spray. Cover with heavy-duty plastic wrap, and microwave at HIGH for 4 to 4½ minutes or until vegetables are tender; drain off liquid. Set onion mixture aside.
2. Place spinach on paper towels, and squeeze until barely moist. Add spinach, cheese, chili sauce, basil, lemon rind, and salt to onion mixture, stirring well. Set aside.
3. Place each chicken breast half between 2 sheets of heavy-duty plastic wrap; flatten to ¼-inch thickness, using a meat mallet or rolling pin. Place ¼ cup spinach mixture in center of each chicken piece. Roll up lengthwise, and secure with a wooden pick. Place rolls, seam side down, in casserole dish recoated with cooking spray.

---

4. Combine tomatoes, ⅓ cup finely chopped onion, garlic, Italian herb seasoning, and pepper; spoon evenly over chicken rolls. Cover with wax paper, and microwave at HIGH for 12 to 14 minutes or until chicken is done, rotating dish after 5 minutes and rearranging rolls so that uncooked portions are to outside of dish.
5. Transfer chicken to a warm platter. Stir 2 tablespoons tomato sauce into liquid in dish. Cover and microwave at HIGH for 1½ to 2 minutes or until thoroughly heated. Pour over chicken; serve immediately.

BAKED CHICKEN
Yield: 4 servings

EACH SERVING Amount: 1 breast half with ¼ sauce

Exchanges: 2 Lean Meat	**Calories:** 96	**Fat:** 1 gm
1 Vegetable	**Carbo:** 6 gm	**Fiber:** 1 gm
Chol: 48 mg	**Protein:** 15 gm	**Sodium:** 207 mg

INGREDIENTS:
4 (3-ounce) skinned, boned chicken breast halves
Vegetable cooking spray
1 (12-ounce) can whole tomatoes, undrained and chopped
½ cup chopped green pepper
½ cup chopped onion
½ teaspoon garlic powder
¼ teaspoon dried whole basil
¼ teaspoon dried whole oregano
¼ teaspoon pepper

STEPS IN PREPARATION:
1. Arrange chicken breast halves in a 10- x 6- x 2-inch baking dish coated with cooking spray.
2. Combine tomatoes and remaining ingredients, stirring until well combined; spoon over chicken in dish. Cover and bake at 400° for 1 hour or until chicken is done.

LEMON CHICKEN
Yield: 14 servings

EACH SERVING Amount: 1 slice

Exchanges: 2 Lean Meat	**Calories:** 75	**Fat:** 1 gm
	Carbo: 1 gm	**Fiber:** Tr.
Chol: 37 mg	**Protein:** 15 gm	**Sodium:** 306 mg

INGREDIENTS:

⅓ cup lemon juice
¼ cup reduced-sodium soy
    sauce
1 clove garlic, minced
½ teaspoon salt

½ teaspoon ground ginger
¼ teaspoon pepper
2 pounds skinned, boned
    chicken breast halves
Vegetable cooking spray

STEPS IN PREPARATION:

1. Combine first 6 ingredients in a shallow container, stirring until well combined. Add chicken; cover and marinate in refrigerator 2 to 3 hours, turning once. Drain and discard marinade.
2. Transfer chicken to rack of a shallow roasting pan coated with cooking spray. Bake at 325° for 1 hour or until chicken is done. Cut into 2-ounce slices.

EXERCISE BREAK: Exercise on a regular basis, and you'll be rewarding yourself in many ways. Research studies show that regular exercise can help you reach and maintain ideal weight, improve the efficiency of your heart and cardiovascular system, strengthen your muscles and bones, reduce anxiety and lift your mood.

CHICKEN CASSEROLE
Yield: 6 servings

EACH SERVING Amount: ½ cup

Exchanges: 1 Medium-fat Meat	**Calories:** 97	**Fat:** 3 gm
1 Vegetable	**Carbo:** 6 gm	**Fiber:** Tr.
Chol: 24 mg	**Protein:** 11 gm	**Sodium:** 376 mg

INGREDIENTS:

4 (3-ounce) chicken breast
    halves, skinned
Vegetable cooking spray
¼ teaspoon salt
¼ teaspoon pepper
½ (10½-ounce) can cream of
    chicken soup,
    undiluted

½ cup skim milk
½ (8-ounce) carton plain,
    unsweetened low-fat
    yogurt
5 unsalted crackers, crushed
1 teaspoon reduced-calorie
    margarine, melted

STEPS IN PREPARATION:

1. Combine chicken breast halves and water to cover in a medium saucepan; cover and bring to a boil. Reduce heat, and simmer 20 minutes or until chicken is done; drain well. Remove chicken from bone; coarsely chop chicken.
2. Place coarsely chopped chicken in a 1-quart casserole dish coated with vegetable cooking spray, and sprinkle with salt and pepper. Combine cream of chicken soup, skim milk, and yogurt in a medium bowl, stirring until well blended; pour soup mixture evenly over chicken.
3. Combine crushed crackers and melted margarine, stirring until well combined. Sprinkle cracker mixture evenly over top of casserole. Bake at 350° for 20 minutes or until thoroughly heated.

CHICKEN SPAGHETTI
Yield: 8 servings

EACH SERVING Amount: 1 cup

Exchanges: 3 Lean Meat	**Calories:** 178	**Fat:** 3 gm
1 Starch	**Carbo:** 15 gm	**Fiber:** Tr.
Chol: 53 mg	**Protein:** 23 gm	**Sodium:** 343 mg

INGREDIENTS:

1½ pounds skinned, boned chicken breast halves
¼ pound uncooked spaghetti
½ (10¾-ounce) can cream of mushroom soup, undiluted
½ cup skim milk
½ teaspoon salt
¼ teaspoon pepper
1 (2-ounce) jar sliced mushrooms, drained
Vegetable cooking spray

STEPS IN PREPARATION:

1. Combine chicken and water to cover in a large skillet; cover and bring to a boil. Reduce heat, and simmer 15 to 20 minutes or until done; drain well. Chop chicken, and set aside.
2. Cook spaghetti according to package directions, omitting salt and fat; drain, and set aside.
3. Combine soup, milk, and seasonings in a small saucepan, stirring to blend.
4. Layer spaghetti, chicken, soup mixture, and mushrooms in a 12- x 8- x 2-inch baking dish coated with cooking spray. Bake at 325° for 30 to 45 minutes or until thoroughly heated.

CALORIE CURB: Sauté poultry and fish in flavored vinegars, leftover cooking liquid from steamed vegetables, or seasoned stock rather than in oil or butter.

CHICKEN CACCIATORE
Yield: 5 servings

EACH SERVING Amount: 1 cup

Exchanges: 2 Vegetable	**Calories:** 113	**Fat:** 2 gm
1 Lean Meat	**Carbo:** 11 gm	**Fiber:** 1 gm
Chol: 28 mg	**Protein:** 13 gm	**Sodium:** 462 mg

INGREDIENTS:

1 tablespoon reduced-calorie margarine

½ pound skinned, boned chicken breast halves

½ cup chopped onion

½ cup chopped celery

1 clove garlic, minced

1 (26-ounce) can whole tomatoes, undrained and chopped

1 cup sliced, fresh mushrooms

½ cup chopped fresh parsley

¼ cup chopped green pepper

1 teaspoon dried whole basil

1 teaspoon dried whole oregano

¼ teaspoon salt

¼ teaspoon pepper

⅛ teaspoon red pepper

STEPS IN PREPARATION:

1. Melt margarine over low heat in a large skillet; add chicken, and cook until lightly browned. Chop chicken, and set aside.
2. Add onion, celery, and garlic to margarine in skillet; sauté until vegetables are tender.
3. Return chicken to skillet with tomatoes and remaining ingredients. Cover and simmer 20 minutes.

Note: Chicken Cacciatore may be served over hot cooked rice or noodles that have been cooked without salt or fat. (Check Exchange Lists for values on rice and noodles.)

CHICKEN CORDON BLEU
Yield: 4 servings

EACH SERVING Amount: 1 chicken roll		
Exchanges: 3 Lean Meat	**Calories:** 172	**Fat:** 6 gm
1 Vegetable	**Carbo:** 6 gm	**Fiber:** Tr.
Chol: 128 mg	**Protein:** 22 gm	**Sodium:** 397 mg

INGREDIENTS:
4 (2-ounce) skinned, boned chicken breast halves

2 (1-ounce) slices cooked lean ham, cut in half

2 (1-ounce) slices low-fat Swiss cheese, cut in half

1 egg, beaten

2 tablespoons all-purpose flour

Vegetable cooking spray

⅓ cup chopped onion

¼ (10½-ounce) can cream of chicken soup, undiluted

STEPS IN PREPARATION:
1. Place chicken between 2 sheets of heavy-duty plastic wrap, and flatten to ¼-inch thickness, using a meat mallet or rolling pin.
2. Place one-half slice each of ham and cheese in center of each chicken breast half. Roll up lengthwise, and secure with wooden picks.
3. Dip each chicken roll in egg and dredge in flour. Place chicken rolls, seam side down, in a shallow casserole dish coated with cooking spray, and bake at 350° for 20 minutes.
4. Combine onion and soup, stirring until well combined. Pour over chicken, and continue to bake at 350° for 15 minutes or until chicken is done.

CHICKEN TORTILLAS
Yield: 6 servings

EACH SERVING Amount: 1 portion

Exchanges: 2 Lean Meat	**Calories:** 162	**Fat:** 4 gm
1 Starch	**Carbo:** 14 gm	**Fiber:** Tr.
Chol: 31 mg	**Protein:** 17 gm	**Sodium:** 682 mg

INGREDIENTS:

2 (4-ounce) skinned, boned chicken breast halves

½ (10½-ounce) can cream of chicken soup, undiluted

½ cup skim milk

½ cup thick and chunky salsa

½ small onion, grated

6 (6-inch) corn tortillas, cut into wedges

1 cup (4 ounces) shredded low-fat process American cheese

Vegetable cooking spray

1½ large canned green chiles, seeded and diced

STEPS IN PREPARATION:

1. Combine chicken and water to cover in a small saucepan; cover and bring to a boil. Reduce heat, and simmer 20 minutes or until chicken is done; drain well. Chop chicken, and set aside.
2. Combine soup, milk, salsa, and onion, stirring to blend. Layer half each of tortillas, chicken, soup mixture, and cheese in a 1½-quart casserole dish coated with cooking spray. Sprinkle with green chiles.
3. Repeat layers with remaining tortillas, chicken, soup mixture, and cheese. Cover and refrigerate 24 hours. Remove cover, and bake at 300° for 1 hour. Divide into 6 equal portions, and serve hot.

NUTRIENT NEWS: Poultry, excluding its fatty skin, is an economical source of protein. Keep in mind that dark meat furnishes about 18% more calories than white meat. However, it's still a good nutritional value because it offers plenty of B vitamins, iron, and calcium at a low-calorie cost.

CHICKEN DIVAN
Yield: 8 servings

EACH SERVING Amount: 1 cup

Exchanges: 2 Lean Meat	**Calories:** 123	**Fat:** 2 gm
1 Vegetable	**Carbo:** 5 gm	**Fiber:** 1 gm
Chol: 46 mg	**Protein:** 20 gm	**Sodium:** 243 mg

INGREDIENTS:

8 (2½-ounce) skinned, boned chicken breast halves
1 (10-ounce) package frozen chopped broccoli
Vegetable cooking spray
¼ (10¾-ounce) can cream of chicken soup, undiluted
¼ (10¾-ounce) can cream of potato soup, undiluted
½ cup skim milk
1½ teaspoons lemon juice
2 tablespoons grated Parmesan cheese

STEPS IN PREPARATION:

1. Combine chicken and water to cover in a large saucepan; cover and bring to a boil. Reduce heat, and simmer 20 minutes or until chicken is done; drain well. Chop chicken, and set aside.
2. Cook broccoli according to package directions, omitting salt and fat; drain well. Arrange broccoli in a 2-quart baking dish coated with cooking spray, and top with chicken.
3. Combine soups, milk, and lemon juice, stirring to blend; pour over chicken and broccoli. Sprinkle cheese over top. Bake at 350° for 25 minutes or until thoroughly heated.

CALORIE CURB: Remember to remove all skin and visible fat from chicken and other poultry before cooking. By doing so, you can cut the fat content by up to one-half.

CHICKEN FLORENTINE WITH MUSHROOM SAUCE
Yield: 2 servings

EACH SERVING Amount: 1 portion

Exchanges: 3 Lean Meat	**Calories:** 180	**Fat:** 5 gm
1 Starch	**Carbo:** 12 gm	**Fiber:** 2 gm
Chol: 42 mg	**Protein:** 24 gm	**Sodium:** 255 mg

INGREDIENTS:

2 (2½-ounce) skinned, boned chicken breast halves

¼ cup chopped onion

Vegetable cooking spray

1 (10-ounce) package frozen chopped spinach, thawed

2 tablespoons (½ ounce) shredded low-fat Swiss cheese

⅛ teaspoon ground nutmeg

½ cup sliced fresh mushrooms

½ cup skim milk

½ cup boiling water

1 tablespoon reduced-calorie margarine, melted

½ teaspoon chicken-flavored bouillon granules

STEPS IN PREPARATION:

1. Place chicken between 2 sheets of heavy-duty plastic wrap, and flatten to ¼-inch thickness, using a meat mallet or rolling pin. Set aside.
2. Sauté onion in a large skillet coated with cooking spray. Remove from heat, and stir in spinach, cheese, and nutmeg.
3. Divide mixture in half, and shape into mounds. Transfer mounds to a 10- x 6- x 2-inch baking dish coated with cooking spray. Top each portion with a chicken breast half. Bake at 350° for 25 minutes or until chicken is done.
4. Place mushrooms in skillet. Stir in milk and remaining ingredients, and bring to a boil; boil 6 minutes, stirring frequently, until liquid is reduced and thickened. Spoon sauce evenly over each portion, and serve hot.

GRILLED MARINATED CHICKEN
Yield: 6 servings

EACH SERVING Amount: 1 breast half		
Exchanges: 2 Lean Meat	**Calories:** 97	**Fat:** 2 gm
	Carbo: 2 gm	**Fiber:** Tr.
Chol: 46 mg	**Protein:** 17 gm	**Sodium:** 219 mg

INGREDIENTS:

3 tablespoons lemon juice
3 tablespoons vinegar
2 tablespoons low-calorie
   mayonnaise substitute
Sugar substitute to equal ¼
   cup plus 2 tablespoons
   sugar

½ teaspoon salt
½ teaspoon pepper
6 (2½-ounce) chicken breast
   halves, skinned

STEPS IN PREPARATION:

1. Combine first 6 ingredients, stirring until well blended; pour over chicken in a shallow container. Cover and marinate in refrigerator at least 1 hour.
2. Remove chicken from marinade, reserving marinade. Grill over hot coals 45 minutes or until chicken is done. Turn and baste every 10 minutes with marinade.

CHICKEN DIJON
Yield: 8 servings

EACH SERVING Amount: 1 breast half		
Exchanges: 2 Lean Meat	**Calories:** 129	**Fat:** 3 gm
1 Vegetable	**Carbo:** 6 gm	**Fiber:** Tr.
Chol: 40 mg	**Protein:** 18 gm	**Sodium:** 353 mg

INGREDIENTS:

½ (8-ounce) carton plain,
   unsweetened low-fat
   yogurt
¼ cup Dijon mustard

8 (3-ounce) chicken breast
   halves, skinned
½ cup soft breadcrumbs
Vegetable cooking spray

STEPS IN PREPARATION:
1. Combine yogurt and mustard, stirring until well blended. Brush breast halves evenly with yogurt mixture, and dredge in breadcrumbs.
2. Arrange chicken in a 12- x 8- x 2-inch baking dish coated with cooking spray. Cover and bake at 400° for 30 minutes.
3. Increase temperature to 450°. Bake, uncovered, for 15 minutes or until chicken is done and coating is browned.

MUSTARDY OVEN-BAKED CHICKEN
Yield: 8 servings

EACH SERVING Amount: 1 breast half		
Exchanges: 3 Lean Meat	**Calories:** 126	**Fat:** 3 gm
	Carbo: 2 gm	**Fiber:** Tr.
Chol: 89 mg	**Protein:** 22 gm	**Sodium:** 279 mg

INGREDIENTS:
8 (3-ounce) chicken breast
   halves, skinned
½ teaspoon salt
⅛ teaspoon pepper
2 tablespoons prepared
   mustard

1 egg
¼ cup plus 2 tablespoons
   grated Parmesan cheese
¼ cup soft breadcrumbs
Vegetable cooking spray

STEPS IN PREPARATION:
1. Sprinkle chicken breast halves with salt and pepper.
2. Combine mustard and egg, beating with a wire whisk until well blended. Combine cheese and breadcrumbs; stir well.
3. Dip chicken in egg mixture, then dredge in breadcrumb mixture. Let stand at room temperature on wax paper 10 minutes to set coating.
4. Transfer chicken to rack of a roasting pan coated with cooking spray. Bake at 400° for 40 minutes or until chicken is done and coating is lightly browned. Transfer chicken to a serving platter.

BOMBAY CHICKEN WITH ALMONDS
Yield: 5 servings

EACH SERVING Amount: ½ cup		
Exchanges: 1 Medium-fat Meat	**Calories:** 116	**Fat:** 6 gm
½ Starch	**Carbo:** 9 gm	**Fiber:** 1 gm
Chol: 12 mg	**Protein:** 8 gm	**Sodium:** 38 mg

INGREDIENTS:

1 teaspoon reduced-calorie margarine

¼ cup chopped almonds

2 teaspoons curry powder, divided

1 cup diced, unpeeled apple

½ cup chopped onion

½ cup sliced fresh mushrooms

1 tablespoon all-purpose flour

1 teaspoon chicken-flavored bouillon granules

1 cup boiling water

½ cup skim milk

1 tablespoon lemon juice

1 cup chopped, cooked chicken

STEPS IN PREPARATION:

1. Melt margarine in a large skillet over medium heat; add almonds. Cook 10 minutes or until almonds are golden brown, stirring frequently.
2. Sprinkle almonds with 1 teaspoon curry powder; toss lightly to coat. Drain almonds on paper towels.
3. Add apple, onion, and mushrooms to skillet; sauté 5 minutes. Stir in remaining 1 teaspoon curry powder and flour. Cook over low heat 2 minutes, stirring frequently.
4. Dissolve bouillon granules in boiling water; add to skillet with milk and lemon juice. Cook over low heat 5 minutes or until smooth and thickened, stirring constantly.
5. Add chicken; continue to cook over low heat, stirring constantly, until thoroughly heated.

CURRIED CHICKEN

Yield: 8 servings

EACH SERVING Amount: ½ cup

Exchanges: 1 Lean Meat	**Calories:** 93	**Fat:** 2 gm
1 Vegetable	**Carbo:** 7 gm	**Fiber:** Tr.
Chol: 23 mg	**Protein:** 11 gm	**Sodium:** 205 mg

INGREDIENTS:

1 large apple, unpeeled and chopped

¼ cup sliced green onions

1 tablespoon curry powder

1 tablespoon water

½ (10¾-ounce) can cream of mushroom soup, undiluted

1 cup skim milk

2 tablespoons minced fresh parsley

2 cups chopped, cooked chicken

½ cup plain, unsweetened low-fat yogurt

STEPS IN PREPARATION:

1. Combine apple, green onions, curry powder, and water in a medium saucepan; cover and cook over medium heat until onions are tender.
2. Add soup, milk, and parsley, stirring until well combined.
3. Add chicken, and simmer 10 minutes.
4. Reduce heat to low, and stir in yogurt. Cook, stirring gently, until thoroughly heated.

Note: Curried Chicken may be served over hot cooked rice that has been cooked without salt or fat. (Check Exchange Lists for value on rice.)

MINI-SNACK: Toss ¾ cup shredded carrots with 1 tablespoon each of raisins and low-calorie mayonnaise substitute. Chill thoroughly. Yield: 1 mini-snack with 87 calories and 1 Starch exchange.

CHICKEN TOSTADA WITH SALSA
Yield: 8 servings

EACH SERVING Amount: ½ tortilla with 2 tablespoons salsa		
Exchanges: 1 Starch	**Calories:** 150	**Fat:** 5 gm
1 Medium-fat Meat	**Carbo:** 17 gm	**Fiber:** 1 gm
Chol: 19 mg	**Protein:** 10 gm	**Sodium:** 154 mg

INGREDIENTS:
1 tablespoon vegetable oil
4 (8-inch) flour tortillas
3 cups shredded lettuce
2 medium tomatoes
¼ cup chopped green
  onions

2 cups shredded, cooked
  chicken
¼ cup (1 ounce) shredded
  low-fat process
  American cheese
1 cup Salsa (see page 180)

STEPS IN PREPARATION:
1. Place oil in a large skillet, and place over medium heat until oil is hot. Add tortillas, one at a time, and cook 1 minute on each side or until thoroughly heated. Cut each tortilla in half.
2. Divide lettuce evenly on top of 8 tortilla halves. Cut each tomato into 8 wedges, and arrange on lettuce. Sprinkle with onions, and top with shredded chicken and cheese.
3. Spoon 2 tablespoons Salsa over each tortilla half.

CALORIE CURB: Next to seafood, poultry is your best bet for limiting saturated fat. Poultry lends itself to such calorie-smart cooking methods as stewing, roasting, braising, grilling, and stir-frying.

CHICKEN CHOW MEIN
Yield: 7 servings

EACH SERVING Amount: 1 cup

Exchanges: 1 Lean Meat	**Calories:** 70	**Fat:** 1 gm
1 Vegetable	**Carbo:** 5 gm	**Fiber:** 1 gm
Chol: 19 mg	**Protein:** 9 gm	**Sodium:** 62 mg

INGREDIENTS:

Vegetable cooking spray
1½ cups chopped onion
1 cup sliced celery
½ cup chopped green
   pepper
2 cups chopped, cooked
   chicken
1 (14-ounce) can Chinese-
   style vegetables, drained

1 (4-ounce) can sliced
   mushrooms, drained
¼ teaspoon ground cumin
1 tablespoon chicken-
   flavored bouillon
   granules
1 tablespoon cornstarch
3 cups water

STEPS IN PREPARATION:

1. Coat a large skillet with cooking spray; place over medium heat until hot. Add onion, celery, and green pepper; cook, stirring constantly, 3 minutes or until vegetables are tender.
2. Stir in chicken, Chinese vegetables, mushrooms, and cumin; cook over medium heat 1 minute.
3. Dissolve bouillon granules and cornstarch in water. Add to chicken and vegetable mixture; continue to cook over medium heat, stirring constantly, until thickened and bubbly.

Note: Chicken Chow Mein may be served over chow mein noodles or hot cooked rice that has been cooked without salt or fat. (Check Exchange Lists for values on noodles and rice.)

CHICKEN-CAULIFLOWER CASSEROLE
Yield: 6 servings

EACH SERVING Amount: ¾ cup		
Exchanges: 1 Lean Meat 1 Vegetable **Chol:** 14 mg	**Calories:** 68 **Carbo:** 7 gm **Protein:** 8 gm	**Fat:** 1 gm **Fiber:** 1 gm **Sodium:** 287 mg

INGREDIENTS:
1 (10-ounce) package frozen chopped cauliflower
½ cup coarsely chopped onion
½ cup water
1 cup skim milk
1 tablespoon cornstarch
1 teaspoon chicken-flavored bouillon granules
½ teaspoon salt
¼ cup (1 ounce) shredded low-fat process American cheese
1 cup chopped, cooked chicken
1 (4-ounce) jar diced pimiento, drained
Vegetable cooking spray

STEPS IN PREPARATION:
1. Combine cauliflower, onion, and water in a medium saucepan; cover and bring to a boil. Reduce heat, and simmer 5 minutes or until vegetables are crisp-tender. Drain well, and set aside.
2. Add milk, cornstarch, bouillon granules, and salt to saucepan, beating well with a wire whisk to blend. Bring to a boil; reduce heat, and simmer, stirring constantly, until thickened and bubbly. Add cheese; stir with wire whisk until cheese melts. Remove from heat.
3. Add cauliflower-onion mixture, chicken, and pimiento to cheese sauce. Spoon mixture into a 1½-quart casserole dish coated with cooking spray. Bake at 325° for 20 minutes or until thoroughly heated.

SQUASH MIX WITH CHICKEN
Yield: 4 servings

EACH SERVING Amount: 1 cup

Exchanges: 1 Lean Meat	**Calories:** 65	**Fat:** 1 gm
1 Vegetable	**Carbo:** 8 gm	**Fiber:** 1 gm
Chol: 12 mg	**Protein:** 7 gm	**Sodium:** 113 mg

INGREDIENTS:

½ cup chopped onion
½ cup sliced celery
1 teaspoon reduced-calorie margarine, melted
2½ cups sliced yellow squash
1 cup sliced zucchini

½ cup chopped, cooked chicken
2 tablespoons water
½ teaspoon salt
½ teaspoon dried whole chervil
⅛ teaspoon red pepper
⅛ teaspoon pepper

STEPS IN PREPARATION:

1. Sauté onion and celery in margarine in a large skillet until tender. Stir in squash and remaining ingredients. Cover and bring to a boil.
2. Reduce heat, and simmer 8 to 10 minutes or until vegetables are tender, stirring frequently. Transfer mixture to a serving dish, and serve hot.

EXERCISE BREAK: To get more out of exercise, try "inside-out" breathing. This breathing technique emphasizes exhaling instead of inhaling. Use your abdominal muscles to consciously push out the old air, and passively let in the new. Exhaling this way makes you flatten your stomach and tuck under your lower backbone which in turn flattens your lower back—an ideal posture for any exercise. Give this technique a try next time you exercise.

BAKED TURKEY-STUFFED TOMATOES
Yield: 6 servings

EACH SERVING Amount: 1 stuffed tomato		
Exchanges: 2 Lean Meat	**Calories:** 114	**Fat:** 2 gm
1 Vegetable	**Carbo:** 7 gm	**Fiber:** 1 gm
Chol: 32 mg	**Protein:** 17 gm	**Sodium:** 379 mg

INGREDIENTS:

6 medium tomatoes
½ teaspoon salt
1 cup skim milk
1 tablespoon all-purpose
    flour
1¾ cups chopped, cooked
    lean turkey

½ cup chopped celery
¼ cup chopped green
    onions
¼ cup (1 ounce) shredded
    low-fat process
    American cheese
½ teaspoon seasoning salt
¼ teaspoon pepper

STEPS IN PREPARATION:

1. Cut tops from tomatoes; scoop out pulp, leaving shells intact. Reserve pulp for use in other recipes. Sprinkle inside of tomato shells with ½ teaspoon salt, and invert on paper towels to drain.
2. Combine milk and flour in a small saucepan, stirring to blend. Bring to a boil; reduce heat to low, and cook, stirring constantly, until smooth and thickened.
3. Stir in turkey, celery, onions, and cheese. Sprinkle with seasoning salt and pepper.
4. Spoon turkey mixture into tomato shells, and place in a 13- x 9- x 2-inch baking dish. Bake at 375° for 15 to 20 minutes or until thoroughly heated.

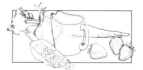

Recipes

Fish and Shellfish

TUNA PILAF
Yield: 4 servings

EACH SERVING Amount: 1 cup

Exchanges: 1 Starch
1 Medium-fat Meat
1 Vegetable
Chol: 19 mg

Calories: 165
Carbo: 21 gm
Protein: 11 gm

Fat: 4 gm
Fiber: 1 gm
Sodium: 364 mg

INGREDIENTS:

1 cup uncooked long-grain rice
1 teaspoon reduced-calorie margarine
2 green onions, chopped
2½ cups water
1 (10-ounce) package frozen mixed Oriental vegetables, thawed

1 (10-ounce) can tuna in water, drained and broken into chunks
1 tablespoon reduced-sodium soy sauce

STEPS IN PREPARATION:

1. Combine rice and margarine in a small Dutch oven. Cook over medium heat 2 minutes or until rice is transparent.
2. Add green onions, and cook 1 minute or until tender. Stir in water.
3. Cover and bring to a boil. Reduce heat to low, and cook 20 minutes or until water is absorbed.
4. Add Oriental vegetables. Continue to cook over low heat 5 minutes or until vegetables are tender.
5. Fold in tuna and soy sauce. Serve hot.

NUTRIENT NEWS: Fish oils continue to show promise. Not only do studies confirm their value in lowering triglycerides in the blood, but for non-insulin dependent diabetics, the omega-3 oils found in fish may increase the body's responsiveness to insulin.

CHOPSTICK TUNA
Yield: 8 servings

EACH SERVING Amount: 1 cup

Exchanges: 1 Starch	**Calories:** 109	**Fat:** 2 gm
½ Lean Meat	**Carbo:** 13 gm	**Fiber:** 1 gm
Chol: 9 mg	**Protein:** 7 gm	**Sodium:** 236 mg

INGREDIENTS:

1 (6½-ounce) can tuna in water, drained and flaked
½ (10¾-ounce) can condensed cream of mushroom soup, undiluted
½ cup skim milk
¼ cup water
1 (10-ounce) package frozen English peas

1 (8-ounce) can sliced water chestnuts, undrained
1½ ounces chow mein noodles, divided
1 medium tomato, diced
½ cup chopped celery
¼ cup sliced green onions
2 tablespoons reduced-sodium soy sauce
Vegetable cooking spray

STEPS IN PREPARATION:

1. Place tuna in a medium mixing bowl.
2. Combine soup, milk, and water; add to tuna, stirring well. Add frozen peas, water chestnuts, half of noodles, tomato, celery, green onions, and soy sauce. Toss lightly to mix.
3. Spoon mixture into a 1½-quart casserole dish coated with cooking spray, and top with remaining noodles.
4. Bake at 375° for 25 to 30 minutes or until thoroughly heated.

Microwave Note: Microwave at HIGH for 5 minutes; rotate dish a half turn, and microwave at MEDIUM (50% power) for 3 to 5 minutes or until thoroughly heated.

STIR-FRIED TUNA

Yield: 6 servings

EACH SERVING Amount: ¾ cup

Exchanges: 1 Lean Meat	**Calories:** 82	**Fat:** 1 gm
½ Starch	**Carbo:** 8 gm	**Fiber:** 1 gm
Chol: 21 mg	**Protein:** 10 gm	**Sodium:** 319 mg

INGREDIENTS:

Vegetable cooking spray
1 medium-size sweet red or green pepper, coarsely chopped
8 green onions, cut into ½-inch slices
1 clove garlic, minced
1 cup diagonally sliced celery
1 (8-ounce) can sliced water chestnuts, drained
5 ounces fresh snow pea pods
2 ounces fresh mushrooms, sliced
1 tablespoon cornstarch
3 tablespoons reduced-sodium soy sauce
3 tablespoons water
1 tablespoon vinegar
¼ teaspoon ground ginger
2 (6½-ounce) cans tuna in water, drained and flaked

STEPS IN PREPARATION:

1. Coat a wok or large, heavy skillet with cooking spray; heat at medium high (325°) for 2 minutes. Add pepper, green onions, and garlic; stir-fry 15 seconds. Add celery, water chestnuts, snow peas, and mushrooms. Stir-fry 1 minute or until vegetables are crisp-tender.
2. Combine cornstarch and next 4 ingredients, stirring until dissolved; add to wok. Cook over high heat (350°), stirring frequently, until sauce is slightly thickened. Add tuna, stirring to coat well.

Note: Stir-Fried Tuna may be served over hot cooked rice that has been cooked without salt or fat. (Check Exchange Lists for value on rice.)

BAKED SALMON
Yield: 4 steaks

EACH SERVING Amount: 1 steak

Exchanges: 2 Lean Meat	**Calories:** 92	**Fat:** 3 gm
	Carbo: 1 gm	**Fiber:** 0 gm
Chol: 26 mg	**Protein:** 15 gm	**Sodium:** 50 mg

INGREDIENTS:
4 (2½-ounce) salmon steaks
Vegetable cooking spray
2 tablespoons lemon juice
½ teaspoon dried whole
  dillweed

½ teaspoon dried parsley
  flakes
½ teaspoon pepper

STEPS IN PREPARATION:
1. Rinse steaks thoroughly in cold water; pat dry with paper towels.
2. Place steaks in a shallow baking pan coated with cooking spray; brush with lemon juice. Sprinkle evenly with dillweed, parsley, and pepper.
3. Bake at 350° for 25 to 35 minutes or until fish flakes easily when tested with a fork.

HELPFUL HINT: When dining out, don't hesitate to ask questions about how foods are prepared. Select simply prepared foods and avoid rich foods that contain many ingredients. Ask for condiments to be served on the side. By requesting that margarine, salad dressings, gravy, sauces, and sour cream be served separately, you can control the amount you use.

SALMON HASH
Yield: 6 servings

EACH SERVING Amount: ½ cup

Exchanges: 1 Medium-fat Meat	**Calories:** 111	**Fat:** 5 gm
½ Starch	**Carbo:** 9 gm	**Fiber:** Tr.
Chol: 10 mg	**Protein:** 7 gm	**Sodium:** 271 mg

INGREDIENTS:

1 (15½-ounce) can red salmon, drained

2 cups finely chopped peeled potatoes

2 tablespoons reduced-calorie margarine, melted

3 green onions, finely chopped

⅛ teaspoon pepper

STEPS IN PREPARATION:
1. Remove and discard skin and bones from salmon; flake salmon with a fork, and set aside.
2. Sauté potatoes in margarine in a large skillet 15 minutes or until tender. Remove from skillet, and set aside.
3. Add green onions to skillet, and sauté 2 to 3 minutes. Stir in pepper.
4. Add potatoes and salmon. Cook over medium heat, without stirring, until thoroughly heated.

NUTRIENT NEWS: Scientists now report that omega-3 "fish oils" can be found in beans, nuts, oils, wheat germ, and even radish sprouts. However, scientists debate how well the human body is able to convert omega-3's from plants to the biologically active form derived from fish. So keep eating your salmon, but remember, no matter how healthy fish oils are, they are still 100% fat and need to be calculated in your meal plan.

STUFFED FLOUNDER FILLETS
Yield: 4 servings

EACH SERVING Amount: 1 stuffed fillet

Exchanges: 3 Lean Meat	**Calories:** 199	**Fat:** 8 gm
1 Vegetable	**Carbo:** 4 gm	**Fiber:** Tr.
Chol: 78 mg	**Protein:** 26 gm	**Sodium:** 259 mg

INGREDIENTS:

4 (2½-ounce) flounder fillets
Vegetable cooking spray
½ cup finely chopped onion
1 clove garlic, minced
¼ cup finely chopped celery
¼ cup finely chopped carrot
¼ cup minced sweet red
   pepper
⅛ teaspoon ground thyme

2 tablespoons chopped fresh
   parsley, divided
1 tablespoon grated
   Parmesan cheese
1 tablespoon low-calorie
   mayonnaise substitute
½ teaspoon Dijon mustard
1 tablespoon lemon juice

STEPS IN PREPARATION:

1. Rinse fillets thoroughly in cold water; pat dry with paper towels. Set aside.
2. Coat a medium skillet with cooking spray; place over medium heat until hot. Add onion and garlic; sauté until tender. Add celery, carrot, and pepper; cover and cook over medium-low heat, stirring occasionally, 5 minutes or until vegetables are tender. Stir in thyme, and cook over medium-high heat until all moisture has evaporated; stir in 1 tablespoon parsley.
3. Spoon an equal amount of mixture in center of each fillet; roll up lengthwise, and secure with a wooden pick. Place rolls, seam side down, in a shallow casserole dish coated with cooking spray.
4. Combine cheese, mayonnaise substitute, and mustard; spread mixture evenly over rolls, and sprinkle with lemon juice. Bake at 400° for 20 minutes or until fish is lightly browned and flakes easily when tested with a fork. Sprinkle with remaining 1 tablespoon parsley, and serve.

CURRIED FLOUNDER FILLETS
Yield: 8 servings

EACH SERVING Amount: 1 fillet

Exchanges: 2 Lean Meat	**Calories:** 127	**Fat:** 5 gm
	Carbo: 1 gm	**Fiber:** Tr.
Chol: 51 mg	**Protein:** 17 gm	**Sodium:** 151 mg

INGREDIENTS:

8 (3-ounce) flounder fillets
2 green onions, minced
2 small cloves garlic, minced
⅛ teaspoon curry powder
⅛ teaspoon red pepper

2 tablespoons all-purpose
   flour
1 tablespoon
   reduced-calorie
   margarine

STEPS IN PREPARATION:

1. Rinse fillets thoroughly in cold water; pat dry with paper towels, and place in a shallow baking dish.
2. Combine green onions, garlic, curry powder, and pepper; rub over surface of fillets. Cover and refrigerate 1 hour.
3. Remove fillets from refrigerator, and coat with flour.
4. Melt margarine in baking dish in a 350° oven; add fillets, turning once. Bake at 350° for 5 to 10 minutes or until fish flakes easily when tested with a fork.

EXERCISE BREAK: Since repetitive aerobic activities, such as running, swimming, and biking can be performed with little concentration on the activity, your brain can be freed to plan projects, solve problems, or better yet, daydream. Your workouts are revitalized because your mind is active, too.

LEMON-BAKED SOLE

Yield: 4 servings

EACH SERVING Amount: 1 fillet

Exchanges: 2 Lean Meat	**Calories:** 92	**Fat:** 1 gm
	Carbo: 3 gm	**Fiber:** 0 gm
Chol: 50 mg	**Protein:** 16 gm	**Sodium:** 79 mg

INGREDIENTS:

4 (3¼-ounce) sole fillets
2 teaspoons reduced-calorie
   margarine, melted
2 teaspoons lemon juice
2 tablespoons all-purpose
   flour

2 teaspoons chopped fresh
   parsley
⅛ teaspoon pepper
⅛ teaspoon paprika

STEPS IN PREPARATION:

1. Rinse fillets thoroughly in cold water; pat dry with paper towels, and set aside.
2. Combine melted margarine and lemon juice in a small bowl. Combine flour, chopped parsley, and pepper in a shallow container. Dip fillets in margarine mixture, and dredge in flour mixture.
3. Transfer fillets to a nonstick baking sheet, and drizzle any remaining margarine mixture over fish. Sprinkle fillets with paprika.
4. Bake at 375° for 15 to 20 minutes or until fish is golden brown and flakes easily when tested with a fork.

Note: If a crisper texture is desired, broil baked fillets 4 inches from heat for 1 minute. Garnish each fillet with a lemon wedge and fresh parsley sprigs, if desired.

HALIBUT FLORENTINE
Yield: 8 servings

EACH SERVING **Amount:** ½ fillet with ⅛ spinach and sauce		
Exchanges: 2 Lean Meat	**Calories:** 109	**Fat:** 3 gm
1 Vegetable	**Carbo:** 5 gm	**Fiber:** Tr.
Chol: 64 mg	**Protein:** 16 gm	**Sodium:** 110 mg

INGREDIENTS:

1 (10-ounce) package frozen chopped spinach

2 tablespoons lemon juice

4 (¼-pound) halibut fillets

1 tablespoon reduced-calorie margarine

2 tablespoons all-purpose flour

1 cup skim milk

1 egg yolk, beaten

¼ cup (1 ounce) shredded low-fat Swiss cheese

1 tablespoon grated Parmesan cheese

STEPS IN PREPARATION:

1. Cook spinach according to package directions, omitting salt. Drain well, and place in a 12- x 8- x 2-inch casserole dish; sprinkle with lemon juice.
2. Rinse fillets thoroughly in cold water; pat dry with paper towels, and arrange on spinach.
3. Melt margarine in a small saucepan over low heat; add flour, stirring until smooth. Cook 1 minute, stirring constantly. Gradually add milk; cook over medium heat, stirring constantly, until mixture is thickened and bubbly. Remove from heat, and stir in egg yolk. Add shredded Swiss cheese, and cook over low heat, stirring frequently, until cheese melts.
4. Spoon sauce over fish, and sprinkle with Parmesan cheese. Bake at 350° for 20 minutes or until fish flakes easily when tested with a fork.

BAKED HALIBUT
Yield: 16 servings

EACH SERVING Amount: ½ steak

Exchanges: 2 Lean Meat	Calories: 66	Fat: 1 gm
	Carbo: 0 gm	Fiber: 0 gm
Chol: 31 mg	Protein: 13 gm	Sodium: 45 mg

INGREDIENTS:

8 (4-ounce) halibut steaks
1 tablespoon Dijon mustard
¼ cup lemon juice
1 tablespoon vinegar
½ teaspoon dried whole
  oregano
¼ teaspoon pepper

½ cup water
½ teaspoon chicken-flavored
  bouillon granules
2 green onions, chopped
2 tablespoons grated
  Parmesan cheese

STEPS IN PREPARATION:

1. Rinse steaks thoroughly in cold water; pat dry with paper towels, and place in a shallow baking dish. Brush steaks evenly with mustard.
2. Combine lemon juice, vinegar, oregano, and pepper. Pour over steaks, and marinate in refrigerator for 1 to 2 hours.
3. Combine water and bouillon granules in a small saucepan. Cook over medium heat, stirring constantly, until bouillon granules dissolve; pour around steaks in dish. Top steaks with green onions and cheese.
4. Bake at 375° for 25 minutes or until fish flakes easily when tested with a fork.

MINI-SNACK: Combine ½ cup each of chopped sweet red and green pepper, ½ cup sliced cucumber, and 1 tablespoon chopped scallions in a small bowl. Add ⅓ cup commercial low-calorie Italian salad dressing, tossing lightly to coat well. Yield: 2 mini-snacks with 32 calories and 1 Vegetable exchange per mini-snack.

VEGETABLE-TOPPED FISH FILLETS
Yield: 6 servings

EACH SERVING Amount: 1 fillet		
Exchanges: 3 Lean Meat 1 Vegetable **Chol:** 64 mg	**Calories:** 154 **Carbo:** 4 gm **Protein:** 24 gm	**Fat:** 4 gm **Fiber:** Tr. **Sodium:** 407 mg

INGREDIENTS:
6 (4-ounce) snapper or cod
    fillets
½ teaspoon dried whole
    tarragon
¼ teaspoon salt
¼ teaspoon pepper
Vegetable cooking spray
1 medium onion
¼ pound fresh mushrooms,
    sliced

3 tablespoons
    reduced-calorie
    margarine, melted
1 medium tomato, seeded
    and chopped
¼ cup low-calorie catsup
2 tablespoons grated
    Parmesan cheese

STEPS IN PREPARATION:
1. Rinse fillets thoroughly in cold water; pat dry with paper towels.
2. Sprinkle fillets with tarragon, salt, and pepper, and place in a 13- x 9- x 2-inch baking pan coated with cooking spray. Bake, uncovered, at 500° for 10 to 12 minutes or until fish flakes easily when tested with a fork.
3. Sauté onion and mushrooms in margarine in a large skillet until vegetables are tender. Remove from heat, and stir in tomato and catsup.
4. Remove fillets from oven; drain off juices. Spoon onion mixture evenly over each fillet, and sprinkle with cheese. Broil 4 inches from heat until cheese begins to melt. Serve immediately.

SHRIMP-MACARONI SALAD

Yield: 12 servings

EACH SERVING Amount: ¾ cup

Exchanges: 1 Lean Meat	**Calories:** 83	**Fat:** 1 gm
½ Starch	**Carbo:** 9 gm	**Fiber:** Tr.
Chol: 48 mg	**Protein:** 8 gm	**Sodium:** 91 mg

INGREDIENTS:

¾ cup uncooked shell macaroni

¾ pound cooked, cleaned medium-size fresh shrimp

1 cup chopped cauliflower

1 cup sliced celery

½ cup commercial low-calorie French dressing

¼ cup chopped fresh parsley

¼ cup chopped sweet pickle

¼ cup low-calorie mayonnaise substitute

1 tablespoon lemon juice

1 teaspoon grated onion

½ teaspoon celery seeds

¼ teaspoon pepper

STEPS IN PREPARATION:

1. Cook macaroni according to package directions, omitting salt and fat. Drain.
2. Combine macaroni and remaining ingredients; toss gently to mix.
3. Cover and refrigerate at least 8 hours. Serve cold.

CALORIE CURB: Substitute stock for oil in marinades. This is a perfect substitution for marinades used for baked fish or salads. Since stock is a good substitution, it can be kept on hand conveniently frozen in ice cube trays. Before freezing, defat stock first by refrigerating and skimming hardened fat from the surface. To use, just remove the number of frozen cubes needed, and thaw them completely.

SHRIMP-STUFFED NOODLES
Yield: 6 servings

EACH SERVING Amount: 1 stuffed noodle		
Exchanges: 1½ Starch	**Calories:** 165	**Fat:** 2 gm
1 Lean Meat	**Carbo:** 24 gm	**Fiber:** 1 gm
Chol: 67 mg	**Protein:** 12 gm	**Sodium:** 169 mg

INGREDIENTS:

6 uncooked lasagna noodles
Vegetable cooking spray
1 clove garlic, minced
1 (9-ounce) package frozen
    French-style green
    beans, thawed
½ cup shredded carrot
2 green onions, thinly sliced

1 cup sliced fresh mush-
    rooms
¼ cup Worcestershire sauce
2 tablespoons Dijon mustard
2 teaspoons cornstarch
1 (6-ounce) package frozen
    shrimp, thawed

STEPS IN PREPARATION:

1. Cook noodles according to package directions, omitting salt and fat; drain well. Set aside, and keep warm.
2. Coat a wok or a large heavy skillet with cooking spray. Heat at high (350°) for 2 minutes. Stir-fry garlic 15 seconds. Add green beans, carrot, and green onions; stir-fry 30 seconds. Add mushrooms, and stir-fry 1 minute or until vegetables are crisp-tender.
3. Combine Worcestershire sauce, mustard, and cornstarch, stirring until dissolved; add to wok. Continue to cook, stirring frequently, until sauce is thickened and bubbly.
4. Add shrimp; stir-fry 1 minute or until shrimp turn pink.
5. Place 1 lasagna noodle on each serving plate; spoon shrimp mixture evenly down the center of each noodle. Fold long ends of each noodle over stuffing. Serve immediately.

SHRIMP AND CHICKEN CREOLE
Yield: 6 servings

EACH SERVING Amount: 1 cup

Exchanges: 2 Lean Meat	**Calories:** 116	**Fat:** 2 gm
1 Vegetable	**Carbo:** 7 gm	**Fiber:** 1 gm
Chol: 97 mg	**Protein:** 17 gm	**Sodium:** 271 mg

INGREDIENTS:

1 cup chopped green
    pepper
¾ cup chopped onion
1 teaspoon vegetable oil
2 cups peeled diced
    tomatoes
½ teaspoon salt
½ teaspoon garlic powder

½ teaspoon chili powder
¼ teaspoon red pepper
⅛ teaspoon pepper
2½ cups uncooked, cleaned
    small fresh shrimp
1 cup chopped, cooked
    chicken

STEPS IN PREPARATION:
1. Sauté green pepper and onion in oil in a large skillet until vegetables are tender.
2. Stir in tomatoes, salt, garlic powder, chili powder, red pepper, and pepper. Bring to a boil. Reduce heat, and simmer, uncovered, 20 to 30 minutes or until mixture thickens.
3. Stir in shrimp and chicken (mixture will thin when shrimp is added). Return to a boil; reduce heat, and cook 1 to 2 minutes or until shrimp turn pink.

Note: Shrimp and Chicken Creole may be served over hot cooked rice that has been cooked without salt or fat. (Check Exchange Lists for value on rice.)

CURRY-SHRIMP CREOLE
Yield: 8 servings

EACH SERVING Amount: ½ cup		
Exchanges: 1 Lean Meat 　　　　　　 1 Vegetable **Chol:** 60 mg	**Calories:** 83 **Carbo:** 7 gm **Protein:** 8 gm	**Fat:** 2 gm **Fiber:** Tr. **Sodium:** 440 mg

INGREDIENTS:

2 medium onions, chopped
1 medium green pepper, cut into 1-inch pieces
1 stalk celery, sliced
1 clove garlic, minced
1 tablespoon vegetable oil
1 (16-ounce) can whole tomatoes, undrained and chopped
¼ cup minced fresh parsley
¼ cup low-calorie catsup
1 teaspoon lemon juice
½ teaspoon salt
½ teaspoon hot sauce
¼ teaspoon curry powder
¼ teaspoon dried whole thyme, crushed
¾ pound uncooked, cleaned medium-size fresh shrimp

STEPS IN PREPARATION:

1. Sauté onion, green pepper, celery, and garlic in oil in a large skillet until crisp-tender.
2. Stir in tomatoes, parsley, catsup, lemon juice, salt, hot sauce, curry powder, and thyme. Cover and bring to a boil. Reduce heat, and simmer 30 minutes.
3. Add shrimp. Cover and simmer 5 minutes or until shrimp turn pink.

Note: Curry-Shrimp Creole may be served over hot cooked rice that has been cooked without salt or fat. (Check Exchange Lists for value on rice.)

SHRIMP STIR-FRY
Yield: 6 servings

EACH SERVING Amount: ¾ cup		
Exchanges: 2 Lean Meat	**Calories:** 121	**Fat:** 3 gm
1 Vegetable	**Carbo:** 7 gm	**Fiber:** 1 gm
Chol: 114 mg	**Protein:** 16 gm	**Sodium:** 370 mg

INGREDIENTS:

1 tablespoon vegetable oil
1 medium onion, thinly sliced
½ cup thinly sliced celery
1 pound uncooked, cleaned medium-size fresh shrimp
6 ounces fresh mushrooms, sliced

½ teaspoon minced garlic
1 cup shredded fresh spinach leaves
¼ pound fresh English peas
1 teaspoon cornstarch
¼ cup water
2 tablespoons reduced-sodium soy sauce

STEPS IN PREPARATION:

1. Coat a wok or large heavy skillet with oil. Heat at medium high (325°) for 2 minutes.
2. Add sliced onion and celery to wok; stir-fry 3 minutes. Add shrimp, sliced mushrooms, and minced garlic; stir-fry 1 minute or until shrimp turn pink. Add shredded spinach and English peas, and stir-fry 30 seconds.
3. Combine cornstarch, water, and reduced-sodium soy sauce, stirring until cornstarch dissolves; add to shrimp mixture in wok. Continue to cook over medium-high heat, stirring just until mixture thickens.

Note: Shrimp Stir-Fry may be served over hot cooked brown rice that has been cooked without salt or fat. (Check Exchange Lists for value on brown rice.)

SHRIMP SCAMPI
Yield: 4 servings

EACH SERVING Amount: 2 ounces

Exchanges: 2 Lean Meat	**Calories:** 91	**Fat:** 3 gm
	Carbo: 1 gm	**Fiber:** 0 gm
Chol: 90 mg	**Protein:** 14 gm	**Sodium:** 107 mg

INGREDIENTS:

1 teaspoon reduced-calorie margarine, melted
1 teaspoon vegetable oil
1 clove garlic, minced
¼ teaspoon pepper

½ pound uncooked, cleaned large fresh shrimp
1 tablespoon chopped fresh parsley

STEPS IN PREPARATION:

1. Combine margarine, oil, garlic, and pepper in a shallow heatproof casserole dish. Add shrimp, and toss lightly to coat. Spread shrimp in a single layer.
2. Broil shrimp 4 inches from heat 3 to 4 minutes. Turn shrimp, and broil an additional 3 to 4 minutes or until lightly browned. Sprinkle with parsley, and serve.

Rice, Pasta, and Starchy Vegetables

PARSLEY RICE
Yield: 8 servings

EACH SERVING Amount: ½ cup

Exchanges: 1 Starch
          1 Medium-fat Meat
Chol: 41 mg

Calories: 136
Carbo: 13 gm
Protein: 10 gm

Fat: 5 gm
Fiber: Tr.
Sodium: 756 mg

INGREDIENTS:

2 green onions, chopped
½ clove garlic, minced
3 tablespoons
     reduced-calorie
     margarine, melted
2 cups hot cooked rice
     (cooked without salt
     or fat)

2 cups skim milk
2 cups (8 ounces) shredded
     low-fat process
     American cheese
1 cup chopped fresh parsley
1 egg, beaten
½ teaspoon salt
Vegetable cooking spray

STEPS IN PREPARATION:
1. Sauté onions and garlic in margarine until tender.
2. Combine sautéed mixture, rice, and next 5 ingredients, stirring well. Spoon mixture into a 1½-quart casserole dish coated with cooking spray, and bake at 350° for 45 minutes.

EXERCISE BREAK: Your level of stamina is determined by diet, exercise, and rest. But, did you know that it is also influenced by your mental attitude? The psychological environment that has proven to be most effective in increasing stamina is rooted in a firm belief in yourself and your abilities.

BLACK BEANS AND RICE
Yield: 6 servings

EACH SERVING Amount: 1 cup beans over ½ cup rice

Exchanges: 2 Starch	**Calories:** 179	**Fat:** Tr.
1 Vegetable	**Carbo:** 36 gm	**Fiber:** Tr.
Chol: 0 mg	**Protein:** 8 gm	**Sodium:** 424 mg

INGREDIENTS:

1 (16-ounce) package dried
black beans

1 medium-size green
pepper, chopped

¼ cup chopped onion,
divided

2½ quarts water, divided

2 cloves garlic, minced

½ teaspoon dried whole
oregano

¼ teaspoon ground cumin

3 tablespoons vinegar

1 teaspoon salt

3 cups hot cooked rice
(cooked without salt
or fat)

STEPS IN PREPARATION:

1. Sort and wash beans. Combine beans, green pepper, and 2 tablespoons onion in a large Dutch oven. Cover with 6 cups of water, and soak overnight.
2. Add remaining 4 cups water to Dutch oven; cover and bring to a boil. Reduce heat, and simmer 2½ hours or until beans are tender.
3. Combine remaining 2 tablespoons onion, garlic, oregano, and cumin in a small bowl; mash mixture, using a fork. Stir in vinegar.
4. Add vinegar mixture and salt to beans. Simmer, uncovered, an additional 20 minutes. Serve over hot cooked rice.

RED BEANS AND RICE
Yield: 8 servings

EACH SERVING Amount: ½ cup

Exchanges: 1 Starch

Chol: 0 mg

Calories: 77
Carbo: 14 gm
Protein: 4 gm

Fat: Tr.
Fiber: 1 gm
Sodium: 189 mg

INGREDIENTS:
Vegetable cooking spray
½ cup finely chopped celery
¼ cup chopped green onions
¼ cup chopped green pepper
1 (16-ounce) can kidney beans, drained
1 teaspoon beef-flavored bouillon granules

1 cup boiling water
1 teaspoon garlic powder
1 teaspoon dried whole oregano
½ teaspoon white pepper
⅛ teaspoon red pepper
1 cup hot cooked rice (cooked without salt or fat)

STEPS IN PREPARATION:
1. Coat a medium-size, nonstick skillet with cooking spray. Place over medium heat until hot. Add celery, green onions, and green pepper; sauté 5 minutes or until tender. Stir in beans.
2. Dissolve bouillon granules in boiling water. Add to sautéed vegetables. Stir in remaining seasonings; bring to a boil.
3. Add cooked rice to skillet, stirring well. Cover and remove from heat. Let stand 5 minutes before serving.

NUTRIENT NEWS: Like all legumes, kidney beans are a good source of protein, iron, B vitamins, and fiber. Combine them with grain products, such as rice, and their protein value increases.

LIMA BEANS DELUXE
Yield: 6 servings

EACH SERVING Amount: ½ cup		
Exchanges: 1 Starch	**Calories:** 116	**Fat:** 2 gm
1 Lean Meat	**Carbo:** 17 gm	**Fiber:** 1 gm
Chol: 4 mg	**Protein:** 8 gm	**Sodium:** 411 mg

INGREDIENTS:

1 (10-ounce) package frozen
    lima beans
1 tablespoon
    reduced-calorie
    margarine
1 tablespoon all-purpose
    flour
1 cup skim milk
½ teaspoon salt

⅛ teaspoon pepper
2 (4-ounce) jars diced
    pimiento, drained
½ cup (2 ounces) shredded
    low-fat process
    American cheese
2 tablespoons low-calorie
    catsup
Vegetable cooking spray

STEPS IN PREPARATION:

1. Cook beans according to package directions, omitting salt and fat. Drain and set aside.
2. Melt margarine in a medium saucepan over low heat; add flour, stirring until smooth. Cook 1 minute, stirring constantly. Gradually add milk; cook over medium heat, stirring constantly, until thickened and bubbly. Stir in salt and pepper. Remove from heat.
3. Add beans, pimiento, cheese, and catsup to sauce; stir well, and spoon into a 1½-quart casserole dish coated with cooking spray. Bake at 375° for 30 minutes or until thoroughly heated.

TWICE-BAKED POTATOES
Yield: 8 servings

EACH SERVING Amount: ½ potato		
Exchanges: 1 Starch	**Calories:** 65	**Fat:** 1 gm
	Carbo: 12 gm	**Fiber:** Tr.
Chol: 2 mg	**Protein:** 3 gm	**Sodium:** 87 mg

INGREDIENTS:
4 small baking potatoes
½ cup skim milk
½ cup plain, unsweetened
   low-fat yogurt

¼ cup (1 ounce) shredded
   low-fat process
   American cheese
½ teaspoon paprika

STEPS IN PREPARATION:
1. Wash potatoes and pat dry; prick each potato several times with a fork. Arrange potatoes end to end and 1 inch apart in a circle on paper towels in microwave oven. Microwave at HIGH for 12 to 14 minutes, turning and rearranging potatoes after 6 minutes. Let potatoes stand for 5 minutes.
2. Cut potatoes in half lengthwise. Scoop out pulp, leaving shells intact. Set shells aside.
3. Mash pulp in a large bowl, using a fork or potato masher. Add milk and yogurt; beat at low speed of an electric mixer until smooth and well blended. Stuff potato mixture into shells, and place on a microwave-safe serving platter.
4. Top each stuffed shell with cheese, and sprinkle with paprika. Microwave at HIGH for 30 seconds or until cheese melts. Serve immediately.

CALORIE CURB: Potatoes are practically fat-free, and are a good source of vitamins, minerals, and fiber. However, it's toppings such as butter and sour cream that can lead you astray. Remember, plenty of B vitamins and potassium can be found in one 3-ounce baked potato for only 80 calories or in one 6-ounce baked potato for 160 calories.

SCALLOPED POTATOES
Yield: 10 servings

EACH SERVING Amount: ½ cup		
Exchanges: 1 Starch	**Calories:** 82	**Fat:** 1 gm
	Carbo: 16 gm	**Fiber:** Tr.
Chol: 1 mg	**Protein:** 3 gm	**Sodium:** 134 mg

INGREDIENTS:
1 clove garlic, minced
1 tablespoon reduced-calorie margarine, melted
1 tablespoon cornstarch
½ teaspoon salt
⅛ teaspoon pepper
1½ cups skim milk
1½ pounds red boiling potatoes, peeled and thinly sliced
¼ cup chopped onion
¼ cup chopped fresh parsley
Vegetable cooking spray

STEPS IN PREPARATION:
1. Sauté garlic in melted margarine in a small saucepan until tender. Stir in cornstarch, salt, and pepper. Add milk, stirring well. Cook over medium heat, stirring constantly, 2 minutes or until mixture is thickened and bubbly. Remove sauce from heat, and set aside.
2. Arrange half each of potatoes, onion, and parsley in bottom of a 2-quart casserole dish coated with cooking spray. Top with half of sauce. Repeat layers with remaining potatoes, onion, parsley, and sauce.
3. Cover and bake at 350° for 45 minutes. Stir once during baking time. Uncover and bake an additional 30 minutes or until potatoes are done.

TARRAGON POTATO SALAD
Yield: 8 servings

EACH SERVING Amount: ½ cup		
Exchanges: 1½ Starch	Calories: 95	Fat: Tr.
	Carbo: 22 gm	Fiber: Tr.
Chol: 0 mg	Protein: 2 gm	Sodium: 62 mg

INGREDIENTS:
1⅓ pounds red boiling potatoes, unpeeled
1 small clove garlic
¾ teaspoon dried whole tarragon
½ teaspoon dried parsley flakes
½ teaspoon dry mustard
½ cup commercial low-calorie Italian dressing
¾ teaspoon lemon juice
2 tablespoons minced green onions

STEPS IN PREPARATION:
1. Combine potatoes and water to cover in a large saucepan; cover and bring to a boil. Reduce heat, and simmer 15 minutes or until potatoes are tender. Drain well, and cool. Cut into ¼-inch slices, and set aside.
2. Combine garlic, tarragon, parsley flakes, and mustard in container of an electric blender. Cover and process 30 seconds or until pureed. Add low-calorie Italian dressing, and process until blended. With blender running, slowly add lemon juice, and continue to process dressing mixture until smooth.
3. Toss dressing mixture with cooked potato slices and minced green onions until well coated. Transfer to a serving bowl, and serve immediately, or cover potato salad and refrigerate for later use.

MACARONI AND PICKLE SALAD
Yield: 8 servings

EACH SERVING Amount: ½ cup

Exchanges: 1 Starch	**Calories:** 101	**Fat:** 2 gm
½ Fat	**Carbo:** 16 gm	**Fiber:** Tr.
Chol: 66 mg	**Protein:** 4 gm	**Sodium:** 283 mg

INGREDIENTS:

1½ cups uncooked elbow macaroni
¼ cup chopped green onions
2 hard-cooked eggs, chopped
2 dill pickles, chopped

½ cup commercial low-calorie Italian dressing
2 tablespoons dill pickle juice
1 tablespoon prepared mustard
1 teaspoon dried whole dillweed

STEPS IN PREPARATION:

1. Cook macaroni according to package directions, omitting salt and fat. Drain and let cool.
2. Combine macaroni, onions, eggs, and chopped pickle in a large bowl.
3. Combine Italian dressing, pickle juice, mustard, and dillweed, stirring to blend. Pour over macaroni mixture; stir well to coat.
4. Cover and refrigerate salad at least 1 hour before serving.

NUTRIENT NEWS: A pasta salad can provide just what is needed in hot weather, something cool, tangy, and refreshing. Pasta has B vitamins, protein, and iron and is considered a low-fat food. However, what goes on the pasta can make it high in fat. To ensure you're getting low-fat fare when dining out, ask your server what's in the salad.

FETTUCCINE ALFREDO
Yield: 8 servings

EACH SERVING Amount: ½ cup		
Exchanges: 1 Starch	**Calories:** 106	**Fat:** 5 gm
1 Fat	**Carbo:** 12 gm	**Fiber:** Tr.
Chol: 16 mg	**Protein:** 4 gm	**Sodium:** 123 mg

INGREDIENTS:
1 (12-ounce) package uncooked fettuccine

3 tablespoons reduced-calorie margarine

1 tablespoon all-purpose flour

½ cup skim milk

¼ cup grated Parmesan cheese

STEPS IN PREPARATION:
1. Cook fettuccine according to package directions, omitting salt and fat. Drain fettuccine well; place in a large bowl, and keep warm.
2. Melt margarine in a medium saucepan over low heat; add flour, stirring until smooth. Cook 3 to 4 minutes, stirring constantly.
3. Gradually add skim milk, and place over medium heat. Cook, stirring constantly, until mixture is thickened and bubbly.
4. Reduce heat to low, and stir in Parmesan cheese. Cook mixture, stirring constantly, until cheese melts and sauce is smooth.
5. Pour sauce over fettuccine, and toss gently to coat. Serve immediately.

CREAMY LINGUINE
Yield: 6 servings

EACH SERVING Amount: ½ cup

Exchanges: 1 Starch	**Calories:** 110	**Fat:** 3 gm
½ Fat	**Carbo:** 15 gm	**Fiber:** Tr.
Chol: 59 mg	**Protein:** 5 gm	**Sodium:** 76 mg

INGREDIENTS:

2 ounces uncooked thin egg
  noodles
2 ounces uncooked spinach
  linguine
3 tablespoons skim milk

1 egg, beaten
¼ cup grated Parmesan
  cheese
1 tablespoon sliced pimiento

STEPS IN PREPARATION:

1. Cook pasta according to package directions, omitting salt and fat. Drain well, and transfer to a large bowl. Keep pasta warm.
2. Combine milk and egg in a small saucepan; cook over low heat 1 to 2 minutes, stirring frequently with a wire whisk. Stir in cheese and pimiento. Remove from heat.
3. Pour cheese mixture over pasta; toss gently until well coated. Serve immediately.

NUTRIENT NEWS: For a healthy pattern of weight loss, consider complex carbohydrates first. Whole-grain cereals and breads, pasta, beans, and vegetables are your best bets because they burn slowly, provide satisfying bulk, help maintain an even blood-sugar level, and give you lots of energy.

FRESH BROCCOLI AND NOODLES
Yield: 8 servings

EACH SERVING Amount: ½ cup

Exchanges: 1 Starch	**Calories:** 107	**Fat:** 3 gm
½ Fat	**Carbo:** 17 gm	**Fiber:** 1 gm
Chol: 17 mg	**Protein:** 4 gm	**Sodium:** 88 mg

INGREDIENTS:

3 ounces medium egg noodles (2 cups)
Vegetable cooking spray
3 cups small broccoli flowerets
2 cups sliced fresh mushrooms
¼ cup chopped onion

¼ teaspoon garlic powder
⅛ teaspoon salt
¼ teaspoon coarsely ground black pepper
3 tablespoons reduced-calorie margarine

STEPS IN PREPARATION:

1. Cook noodles according to package directions, omitting salt and fat; drain and set aside.
2. Coat a wok or a large skillet with cooking spray. Heat at medium high (325°) for 2 minutes. Add broccoli, mushrooms, and onion; stir-fry 4 minutes or until broccoli is crisp-tender.
3. Add garlic powder, salt, and pepper to wok. Stir in cooked noodles and margarine, and continue to cook over medium-high heat, stirring gently, until thoroughly heated.

CALORIE CURB: Vegetables should be cooked without adding fat, such as butter, oil, margarine, bacon, or fatback. Seasoning with a fat product, as allowed on the diet plan, may be done at the table. If a recipe includes fat, the fat must be counted as part of the allowed fat for the meal.

CAULIFLOWER-CARROT PASTA IN CHEDDAR CHEESE SAUCE

Yield: 9 servings

EACH SERVING Amount: ½ cup		
Exchanges: 1 Starch	**Calories:** 80	**Fat:** 1 gm
	Carbo: 13 gm	**Fiber:** 1 gm
Chol: 2 mg	**Protein:** 5 gm	**Sodium:** 238 mg

INGREDIENTS:

2 cups cauliflower flowerets
2 cups diagonally sliced carrots
¼ cup minced onion
2 teaspoons reduced-calorie margarine, melted
1 tablespoon all-purpose flour
1 cup skim milk

½ cup (2 ounces) shredded 40% less-fat Cheddar cheese
¼ teaspoon Worcestershire sauce
⅛ teaspoon salt
⅛ teaspoon pepper
½ cup cooked corkscrew or shell macaroni (cooked without salt or fat)

STEPS IN PREPARATION:

1. Combine cauliflower and carrots in a medium saucepan; add water to cover. Cover and bring to a boil. Reduce heat, and simmer 15 minutes or until tender. Drain well; set aside, and keep warm.
2. Sauté onion in margarine in saucepan 2 minutes or until tender. Add flour, stirring until combined; cook, stirring constantly, 1 minute. Gradually add milk; cook over medium heat, stirring constantly, until mixture is thickened and bubbly.
3. Reduce heat to low, and add cheese, Worcestershire sauce, salt, and pepper; cook, stirring constantly, until cheese melts.
4. Add cooked vegetables and pasta to cheese sauce in saucepan, stirring gently to coat vegetables and pasta well. Continue to cook over low heat, stirring gently, until mixture is thoroughly heated.

SWEET POTATO CASSEROLE
Yield: 6 servings

EACH SERVING Amount: ⅓ cup

Exchanges: 1 Starch	**Calories:** 85	**Fat:** 3 gm
	Carbo: 13 gm	**Fiber:** Tr.
Chol: 44 mg	**Protein:** 2 gm	**Sodium:** 86 mg

INGREDIENTS:

1 (18-ounce) can sweet potatoes, drained
Brown sugar substitute to equal 1 cup brown sugar, divided
¼ cup skim milk
1 egg
1 tablespoon reduced-calorie margarine, melted
1 teaspoon vanilla extract
Vegetable cooking spray
1 tablespoon all-purpose flour
1 tablespoon reduced-calorie margarine

STEPS IN PREPARATION:

1. Combine sweet potatoes, three fourths of the brown sugar substitute, milk, egg, melted margarine, and vanilla, stirring until well blended. Spoon into a shallow baking dish coated with cooking spray.
2. Combine flour and remaining one fourth of the brown sugar substitute; cut in 1 tablespoon margarine until mixture is crumbly. Sprinkle over potatoes, and bake at 350° for 35 minutes or until thoroughly heated.

HELPFUL HINT: Avoid using sauces or creams over vegetables unless they are cal-culated into the meal plan. Instead, use sea-sonings such as bouillon, lemon juice, herbs, spices, or butter substitutes.

POTATO-CHEESE CASSEROLE
Yield: 8 servings

INGREDIENTS:

3 cups cooked, mashed potato

1 egg, separated

½ cup (2 ounces) shredded low-fat process American cheese

½ small green pepper, finely chopped

1 tablespoon finely chopped green onions

½ teaspoon celery salt

1 egg white

Vegetable cooking spray

½ teaspoon paprika

STEPS IN PREPARATION:

1. Combine mashed potato and egg yolk, stirring until well blended. Stir in cheese, green pepper, green onions, and celery salt.
2. Beat 2 egg whites (at room temperature) at high speed of an electric mixer until soft peaks form. Gently fold egg whites into potato mixture.
3. Spoon mixture into a 1½-quart casserole dish coated with vegetable cooking spray. Sprinkle paprika evenly over top of casserole, and bake at 375° for 25 to 30 minutes. Serve immediately.

SEASONED CORN CASSEROLE
Yield: 8 servings

EACH SERVING Amount: ½ cup		
Exchanges: 1 Starch	**Calories:** 80	**Fat:** 1 gm
	Carbo: 16 gm	**Fiber:** 1 gm
Chol: Tr.	**Protein:** 3 gm	**Sodium:** 222 mg

INGREDIENTS:

1 medium-size green pepper, cut into ½-inch pieces
1 clove garlic, crushed
2 teaspoons reduced-calorie margarine, melted
1 tablespoon all-purpose flour
⅔ cup skim milk
¾ teaspoon salt
⅛ teaspoon pepper
⅛ teaspoon dried whole basil
⅛ teaspoon dried whole oregano
1 (16-ounce) can whole tomatoes, drained
1 (16-ounce) can pearl onions, drained
1 (12-ounce) can whole kernel corn, drained
Vegetable cooking spray

STEPS IN PREPARATION:

1. Sauté green pepper and garlic in margarine in a large saucepan until green pepper is tender. Add flour, stirring until smooth. Cook 1 minute, stirring constantly.
2. Gradually add milk and seasonings to saucepan; cook over medium heat, stirring constantly, until mixture is thickened and bubbly. Stir in tomatoes, onions, and corn. Remove from heat.
3. Spoon mixture into a 2-quart casserole dish coated with cooking spray, and bake at 350° for 50 minutes.

MIXED VEGETABLE CASSEROLE
Yield: 8 servings

EACH SERVING Amount: ½ cup		
Exchanges: 1 Starch	**Calories:** 79	**Fat:** 1 gm
	Carbo: 12 gm	**Fiber:** 1 gm
Chol: 4 mg	**Protein:** 4 gm	**Sodium:** 177 mg

INGREDIENTS:

2 (10-ounce) packages
frozen mixed vegetables
½ cup (2 ounces) shredded
low-fat process
American cheese
1 (8-ounce) can sliced water
chestnuts, drained

2 tablespoons chopped
onion
2 tablespoons low-calorie
mayonnaise substitute
Vegetable cooking spray

STEPS IN PREPARATION:

1. Cook mixed vegetables according to package directions, omitting salt and fat. Drain. Combine cooked mixed vegetables, cheese, water chestnuts, onion, and mayonnaise substitute, stirring gently.
2. Spoon mixture into a 1½-quart casserole dish coated with cooking spray. Bake at 350° for 20 minutes or until thoroughly heated.

CALORIE CURB: The safest and most effective way to take off weight is to do it gradually. A loss of 1 or 2 pounds a week—until you reach your goal—is ideal. At first, much of the weight loss will be a loss of water. Real, long-term success depends on your developing new and better habits of eating and exercising.

WILD RICE CASSEROLE
Yield: 10 servings

EACH SERVING Amount: ½ cup		
Exchanges: 1½ Starch	**Calories:** 135	**Fat:** 2 gm
	Carbo: 24 gm	**Fiber:** Tr.
Chol: Tr.	**Protein:** 4 gm	**Sodium:** 833 mg

INGREDIENTS:

1 (10-ounce) package brown and wild rice mix
1 teaspoon salt
1 medium onion, minced
1 medium-size green pepper, chopped
2 tablespoons reduced-calorie margarine, melted
½ (10¾-ounce) can cream of mushroom soup, undiluted
½ cup skim milk
1 (4-ounce) jar whole pimiento, drained and minced
Vegetable cooking spray

STEPS IN PREPARATION:

1. Cook rice according to package directions, using 1 teaspoon salt. Set aside.
2. Sauté onion and green pepper in margarine until tender.
3. Combine cooked rice, sautéed vegetables, soup, milk, and pimiento, stirring well. Spoon into a 1½-quart casserole dish coated with cooking spray, and bake at 350° for 30 minutes.

MINI-SNACK: Combine ¾ cup cubed cantaloupe, ¾ cup cubed honeydew melon and ½ cup vanilla, unsweetened low-fat yogurt; toss lightly to coat well. Top with a sprinkling of unsweetened nutlike cereal nuggets. Yield: 2 mini-snacks with 89 calories and 1 Starch exchange per mini-snack.

VEGETABLE-RICE CASSEROLE
Yield: 10 servings

EACH SERVING Amount: ½ cup		
Exchanges: 1 Starch	**Calories:** 97	**Fat:** 1 gm
	Carbo: 18 gm	**Fiber:** 1 gm
Chol: Tr.	**Protein:** 3 gm	**Sodium:** 182 mg

INGREDIENTS:

2 teaspoons vegetable oil
2 medium-size green
   peppers, cut into strips
1 cup chopped onion,
   divided
2 cups chopped cauliflower
2 cups chopped broccoli
2 cloves garlic, chopped
½ teaspoon dried whole
   thyme

1 tablespoon
   chicken-flavored
   bouillon granules
3 cups hot water
1½ cups uncooked brown
   rice
3 tablespoons
   reduced-sodium soy
   sauce

STEPS IN PREPARATION:

1. Place oil in a large skillet; add green pepper, ½ cup chopped onion, cauliflower, broccoli, and garlic; cook over high heat 5 minutes or until crisp-tender. Stir in thyme. Remove from heat, and set aside.
2. Dissolve bouillon granules in water in a 2-quart casserole dish. Stir in rice, remaining ½ cup chopped onion, and soy sauce. Cover and bake at 350° for 20 minutes.
3. Remove casserole from oven, and stir in sautéed mixture. Cover and bake an additional 10 to 15 minutes or until all liquid is absorbed.

CHICKEN-RICE CASSEROLE
Yield: 8 servings

EACH SERVING Amount: ¾ cup			
Exchanges: 1½ Starch	**Calories:** 157	**Fat:** 2 gm	
1 Lean Meat	**Carbo:** 22 gm	**Fiber:** Tr.	
Chol: 21 mg	**Protein:** 10 gm	**Sodium:** 606 mg	

INGREDIENTS:

Vegetable cooking spray

1 cup uncooked long-grain rice

4 (5-ounce) skinned, boned chicken breast halves, chopped

1 cup water

½ (10¾-ounce) can cream of mushroom soup, undiluted

1 (1.25-ounce) package dry onion soup mix

STEPS IN PREPARATION:

1. Coat a 12- x 8- x 2-inch baking dish with cooking spray. Place uncooked rice in bottom of dish, and top with chicken.
2. Combine water, cream of mushroom soup, and onion soup mix, stirring to blend. Pour over chicken.
3. Cover casserole, and bake at 325° for 1½ hours or until chicken and rice are done.

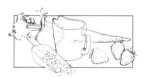

Recipes

Vegetables

ASPARAGUS WITH LEMON SAUCE
Yield: 6 servings

EACH SERVING Amount: ½ cup

Exchanges: 1 Vegetable   **Calories:** 41   **Fat:** 2 gm

                           Carbo: 4 gm   **Fiber:** Tr.

Chol: 44 mg   **Protein:** 2 gm   **Sodium:** 42 mg

INGREDIENTS:

1 (10-ounce) package frozen
    asparagus spears
1 egg
Sugar substitute to equal ½
    cup sugar
½ teaspoon cornstarch

1 tablespoon
    reduced-calorie
    margarine
¼ cup lemon juice
2 teaspoons grated lemon
    rind

STEPS IN PREPARATION:

1. Cook asparagus according to package directions, omitting salt and fat. Drain well. Transfer cooked asparagus to a serving dish, and keep warm.
2. Combine egg, sugar substitute, and cornstarch, stirring to blend. Melt margarine over low heat in a small skillet; add egg mixture. Cook over medium heat until mixture thickens. Stir in lemon juice.
3. Continue to cook over medium heat until thickened and bubbly. Pour over asparagus, and sprinkle with lemon rind. Serve immediately.

BRUSSELS SPROUTS IN YOGURT
Yield: 8 servings

EACH SERVING Amount: ½ cup		
Exchanges: ½ Starch	**Calories:** 51	**Fat:** 1 gm
	Carbo: 8 gm	**Fiber:** 1 gm
Chol: 2 mg	**Protein:** 4 gm	**Sodium:** 42 mg

INGREDIENTS:
2 (10-ounce) packages
   frozen brussels sprouts
½ cup thinly sliced onion
1 teaspoon reduced-calorie
   margarine, melted

1 cup plain, unsweetened
   low-fat yogurt
2 (4-ounce) jars diced
   pimiento, drained

STEPS IN PREPARATION:
1. Cook brussels sprouts according to package directions, omitting salt and fat. Drain and set aside to cool.
2. Sauté thinly sliced onion in margarine in a large skillet. Remove from heat.
3. Add yogurt, pimiento, and brussels sprouts to onion mixture in skillet, stirring well. Cook over low heat, stirring occasionally, until thoroughly heated. Serve warm.

CALORIE CURB: You can reduce the fat content of sauces made with cream and still maintain the velvety, creamy texture by substituting reconstituted instant nonfat dry milk powder made extra strength. Use ½ cup of milk powder to make 1 cup of milk.

COPPER PENNIES
Yield: 6 servings

EACH SERVING Amount: ¾ cup

Exchanges: 1 Starch	**Calories:** 77	**Fat:** 1 gm
	Carbo: 15 gm	**Fiber:** 1 gm
Chol: 2 mg	**Protein:** 3 gm	**Sodium:** 108 mg

INGREDIENTS:

3½ cups sliced carrots
2 medium onions, sliced
2 medium-size green
   peppers, sliced
½ (10¾-ounce) can tomato
   soup, undiluted
½ cup skim milk

½ cup commercial
   low-calorie Italian
   dressing
1 tablespoon prepared
   mustard
1 tablespoon Worcestershire
   sauce

STEPS IN PREPARATION:
1. Cook carrots in boiling water to cover in a medium saucepan until tender; drain and cool. Add sliced onion and green pepper.
2. Combine soup and remaining ingredients; pour over carrot mixture. Cover and refrigerate at least 12 hours.

CHINESE BROCCOLI
Yield: 4 servings

EACH SERVING Amount: ½ cup

Exchanges: 1 Vegetable	**Calories:** 27	**Fat:** 1 gm
	Carbo: 4 gm	**Fiber:** 1 gm
Chol: Tr.	**Protein:** 2 gm	**Sodium:** 79 mg

INGREDIENTS:

1 pound fresh broccoli
Vegetable cooking spray
1 tablespoon reduced-
   sodium soy sauce

1 tablespoon sesame seeds,
   toasted
1 medium-size sweet red
   pepper, sliced

STEPS IN PREPARATION:
1. Trim off large leaves of broccoli. Remove tough ends of lower stalks; wash broccoli thoroughly. Separate broccoli into spears. Peel spears, if desired, and cut into ¼-inch diagonal slices.
2. Place broccoli in a steaming rack. Place rack over boiling water in a large skillet; cover and steam 3 to 5 minutes or until crisp-tender.
3. Coat a large skillet with cooking spray. Add soy sauce, and place over medium heat until hot. Add broccoli; cook 1 to 2 minutes or until tender, stirring constantly.
4. Transfer broccoli to a serving dish. Sprinkle with toasted sesame seeds, and garnish with sliced red pepper.

SKILLET OKRA
Yield: 8 servings

EACH SERVING Amount: ½ cup		
Exchanges: 2 Vegetable	**Calories:** 43	**Fat:** Tr.
	Carbo: 10 gm	**Fiber:** Tr.
Chol: 0 mg	**Protein:** 1 gm	**Sodium:** 208 mg

INGREDIENTS:
1 (16-ounce) can whole
  tomatoes, undrained
  and chopped
1½ cups sliced fresh okra
1 (16-ounce) can
  whole-kernel corn,
  undrained
½ cup chopped onion
½ cup chopped celery
¼ cup chopped green
  pepper

STEPS IN PREPARATION:
1. Combine all ingredients in a large skillet, stirring well.
2. Cover and bring to a boil. Reduce heat, and simmer 15 to 20 minutes.

OKRA FROM THE OVEN
Yield: 8 servings

EACH SERVING Amount: ½ cup		
Exchanges: 1 Vegetable	**Calories:** 30	**Fat:** Tr.
	Carbo: 6 gm	**Fiber:** 1 gm
Chol: 0 mg	**Protein:** 1 gm	**Sodium:** 128 mg

INGREDIENTS:

3 cups sliced fresh okra
Vegetable cooking spray
1 cup chopped tomato
1 cup chopped onion

1 cup chopped green
  pepper
½ teaspoon salt
⅛ teaspoon pepper

STEPS IN PREPARATION:
1. Spread okra in a 13- x 9- x 2-inch baking dish coated with cooking spray.
2. Layer tomato and remaining ingredients over okra. Cover loosely with aluminum foil.
3. Bake at 400° for 1 hour or until okra is tender, stirring occasionally.

PARMESAN PEAS
Yield: 6 servings

EACH SERVING Amount: ½ cup		
Exchanges: 1 Starch	**Calories:** 80	**Fat:** Tr.
	Carbo: 13 gm	**Fiber:** 2 gm
Chol: 1 mg	**Protein:** 5 gm	**Sodium:** 128 mg

INGREDIENTS:

2 (10-ounce) packages
  frozen English peas
1 tablespoon grated
  Parmesan cheese
1 teaspoon lemon juice

1 teaspoon reduced-calorie
  margarine, melted
¼ teaspoon dried whole
  Italian seasoning
⅛ teaspoon grated lemon
  rind

1. Cook peas according to package directions, omitting salt and fat; drain.
2. Toss peas with remaining ingredients, and serve warm.

SPINACH-STUFFED TOMATOES
Yield: 8 servings

EACH SERVING Amount: 1 stuffed tomato		
Exchanges: ½ Starch	**Calories:** 46	**Fat:** 1 gm
	Carbo: 9 gm	**Fiber:** 1 gm
Chol: Tr.	**Protein:** 2 gm	**Sodium:** 226 mg

INGREDIENTS:
8 medium tomatoes
1 (10-ounce) package frozen chopped spinach, thawed
2 teaspoons reduced-calorie margarine
2 tablespoons all-purpose flour

½ teaspoon salt
½ teaspoon dry mustard
¼ teaspoon Worcestershire sauce
2 tablespoons soft breadcrumbs
Vegetable cooking spray

STEPS IN PREPARATION:
1. Cut tops from tomatoes; scoop out pulp, leaving shells intact. Chop and reserve pulp. Invert tomato shells on paper towels; drain 10 minutes.
2. Cook spinach according to package directions, omitting salt and fat. Drain well.
3. Melt margarine in a medium saucepan over low heat; add flour, salt, mustard, and Worcestershire sauce, stirring until smooth. Cook 1 minute, stirring constantly. Stir in spinach and tomato pulp. Remove from heat.
4. Spoon spinach mixture into tomato shells. Top with breadcrumbs, and place in a shallow baking dish coated with cooking spray.
5. Bake at 400° for 15 minutes or until mixture is thoroughly heated and breadcrumbs are browned.

STUFFED BUTTERNUT SQUASH
Yield: 8 servings

EACH SERVING Amount: ½ cup

Exchanges: 1 Starch	**Calories:** 81	**Fat:** 1 gm
	Carbo: 17 gm	**Fiber:** 2 gm
Chol: 0 mg	**Protein:** 3 gm	**Sodium:** 126 mg

INGREDIENTS:

1 medium butternut squash
½ cup water
1 cup finely chopped
    unpeeled apple
¼ cup chopped onion
2 teaspoons reduced-calorie
    margarine, melted

½ cup low-fat cottage
    cheese
¼ teaspoon salt
⅛ teaspoon ground
    cinnamon
⅛ teaspoon ground ginger
⅛ teaspoon pepper
½ teaspoon apple pie spice

STEPS IN PREPARATION:

1. Cut squash in half lengthwise, and remove seeds. Place halves, cut side down, in a 12- x 8- x 2-inch baking dish. Pour water around squash, and bake at 350° for 45 minutes or until squash is tender.
2. Sauté apple and onion in margarine in a large skillet until onion is tender. Stir in cottage cheese, salt, cinnamon, ginger, and pepper. Set aside.
3. Carefully scoop out squash pulp, leaving shells intact. Chop pulp.
4. Add chopped squash pulp to apple mixture in skillet, stirring well. Spoon mixture into squash shells, and sprinkle with apple pie spice.
5. Bake at 375° for 15 minutes or until thoroughly heated.

BAKED SUMMER SQUASH WITH ROSEMARY
Yield: 6 servings

EACH SERVING Amount: 1 cup

Exchanges: ½ Starch	**Calories:** 42	**Fat:** 1 gm
	Carbo: 8 gm	**Fiber:** 1 gm
Chol: 0 mg	**Protein:** 2 gm	**Sodium:** 10 mg

INGREDIENTS:

2 pounds yellow squash
1 tablespoon beef-flavored
    bouillon granules
1 cup hot water

1 teaspoon reduced-calorie
    margarine, melted
½ teaspoon dried whole
    rosemary, crushed

STEPS IN PREPARATION:

1. Cut yellow squash in half lengthwise. Place squash halves, cut side down, in a large shallow baking dish.
2. Dissolve bouillon granules in hot water, and pour bouillon around squash in baking dish. Bake, uncovered, at 350° for 20 minutes.
3. Combine melted margarine and crushed rosemary, stirring well. Turn squash, and baste with margarine mixture. Bake, uncovered, an additional 15 minutes or until squash is tender.

EXERCISE BREAK: For people who exercise heavily on a regular basis, ten glasses of cool, not cold, water per day is the recommended amount to replenish body fluids. Ice cold water is not readily absorbed into the body's tissues.

MARINATED GARDEN VEGETABLES
Yield (includes marinade): 20 servings

EACH SERVING Amount: ½ cup		
Exchanges: 1 Vegetable	**Calories:** 26	**Fat:** 0 gm
	Carbo: 6 gm	**Fiber:** 1 gm
Chol: 0 mg	**Protein:** 1 gm	**Sodium:** 142 mg

INGREDIENTS:

1 medium zucchini, sliced
1 medium cucumber, sliced
2 cups broccoli flowerets
2 cups cauliflower flowerets
2 cups sliced carrots
½ cup chopped green
    pepper
½ cup sliced celery
Garden Vegetable Marinade
    (recipe follows)
4 small tomatoes, cut into
    quarters
1 cup sliced fresh
    mushrooms

STEPS IN PREPARATION:
1. Combine first 7 ingredients in a large bowl. Pour Garden Vegetable Marinade over vegetables. Toss gently to coat.
2. Cover and marinate in refrigerator at least 12 hours, stirring occasionally.
3. Add tomatoes and mushrooms just before serving.

Note: Mixture can be stored in refrigerator up to 1 week.

Garden Vegetable Marinade
Yield (marinade only): 2 cups

EACH SERVING Amount: 2 tablespoons		
Exchanges: Free	**Calories:** 12	**Fat:** Tr.
	Carbo: 3 gm	**Fiber:** Tr.
Chol: 0 mg	**Protein:** Tr.	**Sodium:** 161 mg

INGREDIENTS:

2 cups commercial
    low-calorie Italian
    dressing
Sugar substitute to equal ¾
    cup sugar
2 cloves garlic, crushed
1 teaspoon salt

1. Combine all ingredients in a jar. Cover tightly, and shake vigorously.
2. Store in refrigerator until ready to use as a marinade.

STIR-FRIED VEGETABLES
Yield: 8 servings

EACH SERVING Amount: 1 cup		
Exchanges: 1 Vegetable	**Calories:** 41	**Fat:** Tr.
	Carbo: 8 gm	**Fiber:** 1 gm
Chol: Tr.	**Protein:** 2 gm	**Sodium:** 80 mg

INGREDIENTS:

Vegetable cooking spray
1 clove garlic, crushed
1 tablespoon reduced-sodium soy sauce
3 cups shredded cabbage
2 cups broccoli flowerets
1 cup sliced carrot
1 cup sliced green onions
2 cups sliced fresh mushrooms
1 (6-ounce) package frozen snow pea pods, partially thawed
1 tablespoon cornstarch
2 teaspoons chicken-flavored bouillon granules
1 cup water

STEPS IN PREPARATION:
1. Coat a wok or large skillet with cooking spray. Heat at medium (300°) for 2 minutes.
2. Add garlic and soy sauce; stir-fry 3 minutes.
3. Add cabbage, broccoli, carrot, and green onions. Stir-fry 3 to 4 minutes or until vegetables are crisp-tender.
4. Add mushrooms and snow peas; stir-fry 1 to 2 minutes.
5. Combine cornstarch, bouillon granules, and water, stirring to dissolve. Pour over vegetable mixture, and stir-fry until thickened and bubbly.

CARROT CASSEROLE
Yield: 6 servings

EACH SERVING Amount: ½ cup

Exchanges: ½ Starch	**Calories:** 59	**Fat:** 1 gm
	Carbo: 9 gm	**Fiber:** 1 gm
Chol: 45 mg	**Protein:** 3 gm	**Sodium:** 317 mg

INGREDIENTS:
2 cups cooked, mashed carrots
2 tablespoons (½ ounce) shredded low-fat process American cheese
1 egg, beaten
¼ cup skim milk
½ teaspoon salt
⅛ teaspoon pepper
Vegetable cooking spray

STEPS IN PREPARATION:
1. Combine all ingredients, except cooking spray; stir well.
2. Pour mixture into a 1½-quart casserole dish coated with cooking spray.
3. Bake at 325° for 40 minutes or until thoroughly heated.

ASPARAGUS CASSEROLE
Yield: 8 servings

EACH SERVING Amount: ½ cup

Exchanges: 1 Vegetable	**Calories:** 55	**Fat:** 2 gm
½ Fat	**Carbo:** 5 gm	**Fiber:** Tr.
Chol: 3 mg	**Protein:** 3 gm	**Sodium:** 435 mg

INGREDIENTS:
1 (10-ounce) package frozen asparagus spears
½ (10¾-ounce) can cream of mushroom soup, undiluted
½ cup skim milk
1 (8-ounce) can sliced water chestnuts, drained
½ cup (2 ounces) shredded low-fat process American cheese
Vegetable cooking spray

STEPS IN PREPARATION:
1. Cook asparagus according to package directions, omitting salt and fat; drain and set aside.
2. Combine soup and milk, stirring until blended. Layer half each of water chestnuts, asparagus, soup mixture, and cheese in a 1½-quart casserole dish coated with vegetable cooking spray.
3. Repeat layers with remaining water chestnuts, asparagus, soup mixture, and cheese.
4. Bake at 325° for 20 minutes or until thoroughly heated.

COMPANY CAULIFLOWER CASSEROLE
Yield: 10 servings

EACH SERVING Amount: ½ cup		
Exchanges: 1 Vegetable	**Calories:** 22	**Fat:** 1 gm
	Carbo: 3 gm	**Fiber:** Tr.
Chol: 1 mg	**Protein:** 2 gm	**Sodium:** 88 mg

INGREDIENTS:

1 medium cauliflower, cut into flowerets
Vegetable cooking spray
½ teaspoon salt
⅛ teaspoon pepper
½ cup plain, unsweetened low-fat yogurt

2 tablespoons (½ ounce) shredded low-fat process American cheese
1 teaspoon sesame seeds, toasted

STEPS IN PREPARATION:
1. Cook cauliflower in boiling water to cover in a medium saucepan 8 minutes or until tender. Drain well.
2. Place half of cauliflower in a 1-quart casserole dish coated with cooking spray; sprinkle with salt and pepper. Top with half each of yogurt and cheese.
3. Repeat layers with remaining cauliflower, yogurt, and cheese. Sprinkle with sesame seeds, and bake at 350° for 20 minutes or until thoroughly heated.

CABBAGE CASSEROLE
Yield: 4 servings

EACH SERVING Amount: ½ cup

Exchanges: 1 Vegetable	**Calories:** 58	**Fat:** 2 gm
½ Meat	**Carbo:** 5 gm	**Fiber:** Tr.
Chol: 67 mg	**Protein:** 5 gm	**Sodium:** 342 mg

INGREDIENTS:

1 cup skim milk
1 egg, beaten
¼ teaspoon salt
1 cup grated cabbage

¼ cup (1 ounce) shredded
  low-fat process
  American cheese
Vegetable cooking spray

STEPS IN PREPARATION:
1. Combine milk, egg, and salt in a medium bowl, stirring to blend. Fold in cabbage and cheese.
2. Spoon mixture into a 1-quart casserole dish coated with cooking spray. Bake at 400° for 30 minutes.

ZUCCHINI CASSEROLE
Yield: 8 servings

EACH SERVING Amount: ½ cup

Exchanges: 1 Vegetable	**Calories:** 28	**Fat:** Tr.
	Carbo: 5 gm	**Fiber:** Tr.
Chol: 1 mg	**Protein:** 2 gm	**Sodium:** 16 mg

INGREDIENTS:

4 medium zucchini, sliced
¾ cup shredded carrot
½ cup chopped onion
½ cup water

½ cup plain, unsweetened
  low-fat yogurt
Vegetable cooking spray

STEPS IN PREPARATION:
1. Cook zucchini in boiling water to cover in a medium saucepan 5 minutes or until crisp-tender. Drain well, and set aside.

---

2. Combine carrot, onion, and ½ cup water in a large saucepan. Cover and bring to a boil. Reduce heat; simmer 10 minutes or until crisp-tender. Drain off liquid.
3. Add yogurt and zucchini to saucepan, stirring gently.
4. Spoon mixture into a 1½-quart casserole dish coated with cooking spray, and bake at 350° for 30 to 40 minutes or until thoroughly heated.

SUMMER SQUASH CASSEROLE
Yield: 8 servings

EACH SERVING Amount: ½ cup		
Exchanges: 1 Vegetable	**Calories:** 42	**Fat:** 2 gm
½ Fat	**Carbo:** 4 gm	**Fiber:** 1 gm
Chol: 37 mg	**Protein:** 2 gm	**Sodium:** 360 mg

INGREDIENTS:

1 pound yellow squash
½ cup chopped onion
2 (4-ounce) jars diced pimiento, drained
¼ cup chopped green pepper
1 egg
2 tablespoons low-calorie mayonnaise substitute

1 teaspoon salt
Vegetable cooking spray
2 tablespoons cracker crumbs
¼ cup (1 ounce) shredded low-fat process American cheese

STEPS IN PREPARATION:
1. Cook squash in boiling water to cover in a medium saucepan 15 minutes or until tender. Drain and mash.
2. Combine chopped onion, pimiento, chopped green pepper, egg, mayonnaise substitute, and salt in a medium bowl, stirring well. Stir in squash.
3. Spoon squash mixture into a 2-quart casserole dish coated with cooking spray. Sprinkle with cracker crumbs.
4. Bake at 325° for 30 minutes. Top with cheese during the last 5 minutes of baking time.

GREEN BEAN AND YOGURT CASSEROLE
Yield: 6 servings

EACH SERVING Amount: ½ cup

Exchanges: 1 Vegetable	**Calories:** 42	**Fat:** 2 gm
	Carbo: 4 gm	**Fiber:** Tr.
Chol: 2 mg	**Protein:** 3 gm	**Sodium:** 506 mg

INGREDIENTS:

1 (16-ounce) can
   French-style green
   beans, undrained
Vegetable cooking spray
1 tablespoon chopped onion
1 tablespoon
   reduced-calorie
   margarine, melted
1 tablespoon all-purpose
   flour

½ teaspoon salt
¼ teaspoon pepper
½ cup plain, unsweetened
   low-fat yogurt
¼ cup (1 ounce) shredded
   low-fat process
   American cheese

STEPS IN PREPARATION:

1. Place beans in a small saucepan; bring to a boil. Remove from heat, and drain. Transfer beans to a 1-quart casserole dish coated with cooking spray. Set aside, and keep warm.
2. Sauté onion in margarine in saucepan until tender. Blend in flour, salt, and pepper. Cook over low heat 1 minute, stirring constantly. Remove from heat, and gradually add yogurt, stirring well.
3. Pour yogurt mixture over beans, and sprinkle with cheese. Broil 3 to 4 inches from heat until cheese melts.

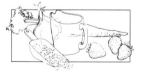

Recipes

Salads

WALDORF SALAD
Yield: 5 servings

EACH SERVING Amount: 1 cup

Exchanges: 1 Fruit	**Calories:** 98	**Fat:** 3 gm
1 Fat	**Carbo:** 18 gm	**Fiber:** 1 gm
Chol: 12 mg	**Protein:** Tr.	**Sodium:** 19 mg

INGREDIENTS:

3 medium apples, unpeeled
 and diced
½ cup sliced celery
¼ cup raisins

½ cup low-calorie
 mayonnaise substitute
1 tablespoon lemon juice

STEPS IN PREPARATION:
1. Combine apple, celery, and raisins in a medium bowl.
2. Combine low-calorie mayonnaise substitute and lemon juice, stirring well to blend. Add to fruit mixture, and toss lightly to coat well.
3. Cover and refrigerate until thoroughly chilled.

FRUIT MEDLEY
Yield: 7 servings

EACH SERVING Amount: ⅔ cup

Exchanges: 1 Fruit	**Calories:** 72	**Fat:** 1 gm
	Carbo: 15 gm	**Fiber:** Tr.
Chol: 2 mg	**Protein:** 2 gm	**Sodium:** 25 mg

INGREDIENTS

1 cup water-packed
 pineapple chunks or
 tidbits
1 cup fresh orange slices
1 cup diced, unpeeled apple

1 cup canned, unsweetened
 drained cherries
1 cup plain, unsweetened
 low-fat yogurt

STEPS IN PREPARATION:

1. Combine pineapple, orange slices, apple, and cherries in a medium bowl. Gently fold in yogurt.
2. Cover and refrigerate until thoroughly chilled.

LIME-COTTAGE CHEESE SALAD

Yield: 10 servings

EACH SERVING Amount: ½ cup		
Exchanges: ½ Skim Milk	**Calories:** 32	**Fat:** 1 gm
	Carbo: 3 gm	**Fiber:** Tr.
Chol: 2 mg	**Protein:** 3 gm	**Sodium:** 57 mg

INGREDIENTS:

1 (0.6-ounce) package sugar-free, lime-flavored gelatin
2 cups boiling water
2 cups cold water
2 tablespoons low-calorie mayonnaise substitute

1 cup low-fat cottage cheese
1 (8¼-ounce) can crushed, water-packed pineapple, drained
Vegetable cooking spray
Lettuce leaves (optional)

STEPS IN PREPARATION:

1. Dissolve gelatin in boiling water in a medium bowl, stirring well. Stir in cold water. Chill until mixture is the consistency of unbeaten egg white.
2. Fold mayonnaise substitute into gelatin mixture. Add cottage cheese and pineapple, stirring well. Pour gelatin mixture into a 6-cup mold coated with cooking spray.
3. Chill gelatin mixture until firm. Unmold salad onto lettuce leaves, if desired. (Check Exchange Lists for value on lettuce leaves.)

STRAWBERRY-PINEAPPLE SALAD

Yield: 10 servings

EACH SERVING Amount: 1 square		
Exchanges: 1 Fruit	**Calories:** 72	**Fat:** Tr.
	Carbo: 16 gm	**Fiber:** Tr.
Chol: 1 mg	**Protein:** 2 gm	**Sodium:** 18 mg

INGREDIENTS:

1 (0.3-ounce) package sugar-free, strawberry-flavored gelatin

¾ cup boiling water

1 (10-ounce) package frozen unsweetened strawberries, partially thawed

1 (8¼-ounce) can crushed, water-packed pineapple, undrained

1 medium banana, mashed

Vegetable cooking spray

1 cup plain, unsweetened low-fat yogurt

STEPS IN PREPARATION:

1. Dissolve gelatin in boiling water in a large mixing bowl, stirring well. Chill until mixture is the consistency of unbeaten egg white.
2. Fold strawberries, pineapple, and banana into gelatin mixture. Pour half of mixture into a 13- x 9- x 2-inch baking dish coated with cooking spray; chill until firm. Store remaining gelatin mixture at room temperature.
3. Spread yogurt evenly over congealed layer. Pour remaining gelatin mixture over yogurt.
4. Chill until firm. Cut into squares to serve.

VEGETABLE CONGEALED SALAD
Yield: 10 servings

EACH SERVING Amount: ½ cup

Exchanges: Free	**Calories:** 10	**Fat:** Tr.
	Carbo: 2 gm	**Fiber:** Tr.
Chol: 0 mg	**Protein:** Tr.	**Sodium:** 16 mg

INGREDIENTS:

1 (0.6-ounce) package sugar-free, lime-flavored gelatin
2 cups boiling water
1¾ cups cold water
¼ cup vinegar
1 cup chopped celery

1 cup shredded carrot
2 tablespoons chopped sweet red pepper
2 tablespoons chopped green onions
Vegetable cooking spray
Lettuce leaves (optional)

STEPS IN PREPARATION:

1. Dissolve gelatin in boiling water in a medium bowl, stirring well. Stir in cold water and vinegar. Chill until mixture is the consistency of unbeaten egg white.
2. Fold in vegetables, and pour gelatin mixture into eight ⅔-cup molds coated with cooking spray.
3. Chill until firm. Unmold onto lettuce leaves, if desired. (Check Exchange Lists for value on lettuce leaves.)

NUTRIENT NEWS: Fresh fruits and vegetables that are eaten raw or slightly cooked are packed with nutrients, yet are low in calories. Use them in salads to provide superior flavor with a satisfying crunch.

SUMMER SALAD
Yield: 10 servings

EACH SERVING Amount: ½ cup

Exchanges: Free	**Calories:** 11	**Fat:** Tr.
	Carbo: Tr.	**Fiber:** Tr.
Chol: 0 mg	**Protein:** 2 gm	**Sodium:** 8 mg

INGREDIENTS:
1 (0.6-ounce) package
    sugar-free, orange-
    flavored gelatin
2 cups boiling water
2 cups cold water

½ cup sliced celery
½ cup carrot curls
½ cup coarsely chopped
    cucumber
Vegetable cooking spray

STEPS IN PREPARATION:
1. Dissolve gelatin in boiling water in a large bowl, stirring
   well. Stir in cold water. Chill until mixture is the
   consistency of unbeaten egg white.
2. Fold in celery, carrot, and coarsely chopped cucumber.
3. Pour into ten ½-cup molds coated with cooking spray, and
   chill until firm.

CARROT-GRAPE SALAD
Yield: 5 servings

EACH SERVING Amount: ½ cup

Exchanges: 1 Vegetable	**Calories:** 38	**Fat:** Tr.
	Carbo: 8 gm	**Fiber:** 1 gm
Chol: 2 mg	**Protein:** 1 gm	**Sodium:** 101 mg

INGREDIENTS:
24 large seedless green
    grapes, halved
2 cups shredded carrot
2 teaspoons low-calorie
    mayonnaise substitute

½ teaspoon poppy seeds
¼ teaspoon salt
5 iceberg or romaine lettuce
    leaves

STEPS IN PREPARATION:
1. Combine grapes and carrot in a large bowl, stirring well.
2. Combine mayonnaise substitute, poppy seeds, and salt; add to carrot mixture, stirring well to coat.
3. Cover and refrigerate at least 2 hours. Serve salad on individual lettuce-lined plates.

APPLE-CAULIFLOWER SALAD
Yield (includes dressing): 6 servings

EACH SERVING Amount: ⅔ cup		
Exchanges: 1 Fruit	**Calories:** 64	**Fat:** 1 gm
	Carbo: 14 gm	**Fiber:** 1 gm
Chol: 0 mg	**Protein:** 1 gm	**Sodium:** 18 mg

INGREDIENTS:
2 large, unpeeled Red
    Delicious apples, thinly
    sliced
1 cup chopped cauliflower

¾ cup Poppy Seed Dressing
    (see page 182)
Lettuce leaves (optional)

STEPS IN PREPARATION:
1. Combine apple slices and cauliflower in a medium mixing bowl. Add Poppy Seed Dressing, and toss lightly to coat.
2. Cover and refrigerate until thoroughly chilled.
3. Serve salad on individual lettuce-lined plates, if desired. (Check Exchange Lists for value on lettuce leaves.)

HELPFUL HINT: If you know you will be eating out, plan ahead. Save your fat exchanges for the meal away from home; this way you can stay within your fat allowances. Do not move the other food exchanges, because moving them affects your blood sugar.

GREEN BEAN SALAD
Yield: 4 servings

EACH SERVING Amount: ½ cup

Exchanges: 1 Vegetable	**Calories:** 32	**Fat:** Tr.
	Carbo: 7 gm	**Fiber:** Tr.
Chol: 0 mg	**Protein:** 1 gm	**Sodium:** 582 mg

INGREDIENTS:
2 (10-ounce) cans cut green beans, undrained
½ cup chopped dill pickles
1 clove garlic, minced
½ teaspoon dried whole basil
½ teaspoon dried whole oregano
1 small red onion, sliced
1 cup commercial low-calorie Italian dressing

STEPS IN PREPARATION:
1. Heat beans in medium saucepan for 5 minutes. Drain.
2. Combine beans and remaining ingredients in a medium bowl; toss lightly to coat. Cover and refrigerate at least 8 hours. Serve salad, using a slotted spoon.

CHILLED CAULIFLOWER SALAD
Yield: 10 servings

EACH SERVING Amount: ½ cup

Exchanges: Free	**Calories:** 18	**Fat:** Tr.
	Carbo: 4 gm	**Fiber:** 1 gm
Chol: 0 mg	**Protein:** 1 gm	**Sodium:** 160 mg

INGREDIENTS:
1 medium cauliflower, broken into flowerets
½ cup sliced celery
½ cup commercial low-calorie Italian dressing
2 small cloves garlic, minced
¼ teaspoon salt
¼ teaspoon pepper
¼ teaspoon red pepper

STEPS IN PREPARATION:

1. Combine cauliflower and water to cover in a medium saucepan; cover and bring to a boil. Cook 4 to 5 minutes or until crisp-tender. Drain.
2. Combine cooked cauliflower and celery in a medium bowl.
3. Combine low-calorie Italian dressing, minced garlic, salt, and pepper, stirring well. Pour dressing mixture over cooked vegetables, tossing gently to coat well. Sprinkle top of salad with red pepper.
4. Cover and refrigerate at least 2 hours.

MARINATED CUCUMBER SALAD

Yield: 5 servings

EACH SERVING Amount: ½ cup		
Exchanges: Free	**Calories:** 21	**Fat:** Tr.
	Carbo: 4 gm	**Fiber:** Tr.
Chol: 0 mg	**Protein:** Tr.	**Sodium:** 5 mg

INGREDIENTS:

½ cup commercial low-calorie Italian dressing
⅛ teaspoon pepper
1 medium cucumber, peeled and thinly sliced
½ small onion, thinly sliced
¼ cup thinly sliced radishes
2 tablespoons chopped fresh parsley

STEPS IN PREPARATION:

1. Combine Italian dressing and pepper in a medium bowl, stirring well. Add cucumber, onion, radishes, and parsley. Toss gently to coat.
2. Cover and marinate in refrigerator at least 4 hours. Serve salad, using a slotted spoon.

MARINATED COLESLAW
Yield: 12 servings

EACH SERVING Amount: ½ cup		
Exchanges: 1 Vegetable	**Calories:** 35	**Fat:** Tr.
	Carbo: 7 gm	**Fiber:** 1 gm
Chol: 0 mg	**Protein:** 1 gm	**Sodium:** 12 mg

INGREDIENTS:
3 cups shredded cabbage
1 large green pepper, diced
1 large onion, diced
Sugar substitute to equal ¾ cup sugar
1½ cups commercial low-calorie Italian dressing
1 tablespoon dry mustard
1 tablespoon celery seeds

STEPS IN PREPARATION:
1. Combine cabbage, green pepper, onion, and sugar substitute in a large bowl; stir well.
2. Combine Italian dressing, dry mustard, and celery seeds in a small saucepan. Bring to a boil, and remove from heat.
3. Pour dressing mixture over vegetable mixture, tossing gently to coat.
4. Cover and refrigerate 1 hour or until thoroughly chilled. Stir coleslaw lightly before serving, and serve, using a slotted spoon.

EXERCISE BREAK: Reluctant to exercise? Try setting goals that are within your reach. Write down your goals, making sure one of them is to exercise on a regular basis. Then begin! Stay motivated by tracking your progress toward your goals.

CALIFORNIA COLESLAW
Yield: 8 servings

EACH SERVING Amount: ½ cup		
Exchanges: 1 Vegetable	**Calories:** 16	**Fat:** Tr.
	Carbo: 4 gm	**Fiber:** Tr.
Chol: 0 mg	**Protein:** Tr.	**Sodium:** 45 mg

INGREDIENTS:
1 cup shredded cabbage
1 cup shredded red cabbage
½ cup shredded carrot
½ cup chopped green
    pepper
½ cup chopped sweet red
    pepper
¼ cup chopped onion

1 tablespoon plus 1½
    teaspoons minced fresh
    parsley
¼ cup vinegar
¼ cup commercial low-
    calorie Italian dressing
Liquid sugar substitute to
    equal ¼ cup sugar
⅛ teaspoon salt
⅛ teaspoon pepper

STEPS IN PREPARATION:
1. Combine cabbages, carrot, green and red peppers, onion, and parsley in a large bowl, stirring well. Set aside.
2. Combine vinegar, Italian dressing, sugar substitute, salt, and pepper in a jar; cover tightly, and shake vigorously.
3. Pour dressing mixture over vegetables, tossing gently to coat well.
4. Cover and refrigerate until thoroughly chilled. Stir coleslaw lightly before serving, and serve, using a slotted spoon.

SPINACH-MANDARIN SALAD
Yield (includes dressing): 10 servings

EACH SERVING Amount: 1 cup		
Exchanges: 1 Lean Meat	**Calories:** 78	**Fat:** 2 gm
1 Vegetable	**Carbo:** 8 gm	**Fiber:** 1 gm
Chol: 13 mg	**Protein:** 8 gm	**Sodium:** 142 mg

INGREDIENTS:
4 cups fresh spinach leaves
2 cups cherry tomatoes
1½ cups chopped, cooked
   chicken breast, chilled
1 cup thinly sliced radishes
½ pound fresh mushrooms,
   sliced

½ cup croutons
Mandarin Dressing (recipe
   follows)
2 tablespoons sesame seeds,
   toasted

STEPS IN PREPARATION:
1. Wash spinach leaves thoroughly in cold water; drain. Remove and discard stems.
2. Place spinach in a large bowl. Add tomatoes, chicken, radishes, mushrooms, and croutons.
3. Add Mandarin Dressing, and toss salad gently. Garnish salad with sesame seeds, and serve on chilled plates.

Mandarin Dressing
Yield (dressing only): ¼ cup plus 2 tablespoons

EACH SERVING Amount: 2 tablespoons		
Exchanges: Free	**Calories:** 21	**Fat:** 1 gm
	Carbo: 3 gm	**Fiber:** Tr.
Chol: Tr.	**Protein:** 1 gm	**Sodium:** 225 mg

INGREDIENTS:
¼ cup commercial
   low-calorie Italian
   dressing
2 tablespoons reduced-
   sodium soy sauce

1 teaspoon vinegar
1 teaspoon sesame seeds
Sugar substitute to equal 2
   tablespoons sugar
⅛ teaspoon pepper

STEPS IN PREPARATION:
1. Combine all ingredients in a jar; cover tightly, and shake vigorously.
2. Refrigerate at least 2 hours to blend flavors. Serve over vegetable salads.

CHEF'S SALAD
Yield (includes dressing): 8 servings

EACH SERVING Amount: 1½ cups		
Exchanges: 1 Medium-fat Meat	**Calories:** 92	**Fat:** 4 gm
1 Vegetable	**Carbo:** 5 gm	**Fiber:** 1 gm
Chol: 44 mg	**Protein:** 9 gm	**Sodium:** 57 mg

INGREDIENTS:

8 cups torn iceberg lettuce
1 cup thinly sliced radishes
2 green onions, sliced
⅓ cup Thousand Island Dressing (see page 183)
2 ounces chopped, cooked low-fat ham
2 ounces chopped, cooked low-fat turkey

2 (1-ounce) slices low-fat process American cheese, diced
1 (1-ounce) slice low-fat Swiss cheese, diced
2 small tomatoes, chopped
1 hard-cooked egg, chopped

STEPS IN PREPARATION:
1. Combine lettuce, radishes, and green onions in a large bowl. Cover and refrigerate until thoroughly chilled.
2. Pour Thousand Island Dressing over vegetable mixture; toss gently to coat. Top with ham, turkey, cheeses, tomatoes, and egg.

TURKEY SALAD
Yield: 6 servings

EACH SERVING Amount: 1 cup

Exchanges: 1 Medium-fat Meat   **Calories:** 96   **Fat:** 4 gm
            1 Vegetable   **Carbo:** 7 gm   **Fiber:** 1 gm
Chol: 109 mg   **Protein:** 9 gm   **Sodium:** 560 mg

INGREDIENTS:

2 medium tomatoes, sliced
1 (10½-ounce) can asparagus spears, drained and chopped
2 cups chopped fresh spinach leaves
5 ounces cooked low-fat turkey, cut into ½-inch strips

2 hard-cooked eggs, chopped
1 green onion, chopped
¼ cup plus 2 tablespoons commercial low-calorie Italian dressing
¼ cup prepared mustard

STEPS IN PREPARATION:

1. Combine tomatoes, asparagus, spinach, turkey, eggs, and green onion in a large bowl. Cover and refrigerate until thoroughly chilled.
2. Combine Italian dressing and mustard, stirring until blended. Pour over salad, and toss gently to coat.

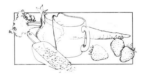

Recipes

Sauces, Toppings, and Dressings

MEATLESS TOMATO SAUCE
YIELD: 4 servings

	EACH SERVING Amount: ½ cup	
Exchanges: 1 Vegetable	**Calories:** 25	**Fat:** Tr.
	Carbo: 5 gm	**Fiber:** Tr.
Chol: 0 mg	**Protein:** 1 gm	**Sodium:** 253 mg

INGREDIENTS:

1 (16-ounce) can low-sodium whole tomatoes, undrained and chopped
1 tablespoon dried whole basil
1 teaspoon garlic powder
½ teaspoon salt
⅛ teaspoon pepper

STEPS IN PREPARATION:
1. Combine all ingredients in a medium saucepan, stirring until well blended.
2. Bring tomato mixture to a boil; reduce heat, and simmer, uncovered, 30 minutes, stirring occasionally.

Note: Meatless Tomato Sauce may be served over hot cooked noodles that have been cooked without salt or fat. (Check Exchange Lists for value on noodles.)

BARBECUE SAUCE
Yield: 5 servings

	EACH SERVING Amount: ½ cup	
Exchanges: Free	**Calories:** 13	**Fat:** Tr.
	Carbo: 3 gm	**Fiber:** 0 gm
Chol: 0 mg	**Protein:** Tr.	**Sodium:** 19 mg

INGREDIENTS:

2 cups diet cola-flavored carbonated beverage
½ cup low-calorie catsup

STEPS IN PREPARATION:
1. Combine carbonated beverage and catsup, stirring until well blended.
2. Store in an airtight container in refrigerator.

Note: Barbecue Sauce may be used as a marinating or basting sauce for meat. (Check Exchange Lists for value on meat.)

MOCK SOUR CREAM
Yield: 18 servings

EACH SERVING Amount: 1 tablespoon		
Exchanges: Free	**Calories:** 11	**Fat:** Tr.
	Carbo: 1 gm	**Fiber:** 0 gm
Chol: Tr.	**Protein:** 2 gm	**Sodium:** 31 mg

INGREDIENTS:
1 cup low-fat cottage cheese   1 tablespoon lemon juice
2 tablespoons skim milk

STEPS IN PREPARATION:
1. Combine all ingredients in container of an electric blender; cover and process until smooth and creamy.
2. Transfer mixture to a serving container; cover and refrigerate until thoroughly chilled.

Note: Mock Sour Cream may be used as a sour cream substitute to top baked potatoes or tostadas. (Check Exchange Lists for values on potatoes and tostadas.)

HELPFUL HINT: Pureed vegetables or fruits, such as carrots, mushrooms, spinach, broccoli, leeks, and watercress, can actually be the thickening base of a sauce. They provide excellent flavoring and good body.

SALSA
Yield: 1 cup

EACH SERVING Amount: 2 tablespoons

Exchanges: Free	**Calories:** 14	**Fat:** 1 gm
	Carbo: 2 gm	**Fiber:** Tr.
Chol: 0 mg	**Protein:** Tr.	**Sodium:** 124 mg

INGREDIENTS:
2 medium tomatoes, peeled
   and chopped
3 tablespoons canned, diced
   green chiles, drained

2 tablespoons minced onion
1 teaspoon vegetable oil
1 teaspoon vinegar
½ teaspoon salt

STEPS IN PREPARATION:
1. Combine all ingredients, stirring well.
2. Transfer mixture to a serving container. Cover and refrigerate until thoroughly chilled.

Note: Salsa may be served with tortilla chips as an appetizer. (Check Exchange Lists for value on chips.)

GUACAMOLE
Yield: 12 servings

EACH SERVING Amount: 2 tablespoons

Exchanges: 1 Fat	**Calories:** 38	**Fat:** 3 gm
	Carbo: 2 gm	**Fiber:** 1 gm
Chol: 0 mg	**Protein:** Tr.	**Sodium:** 43 mg

INGREDIENTS:
2 large avocados, peeled,
   seeded, and mashed
3 medium-size canned green
   chiles, seeded and
   chopped

3 tablespoons lemon or lime
   juice
¼ teaspoon salt

STEPS IN PREPARATION:
1. Combine avocados and green chiles in a medium bowl, stirring to blend.
2. Add lemon juice and salt, stirring well. Cover and refrigerate until thoroughly chilled.

Note: Guacamole may be used to top shredded lettuce. (Check Exchange Lists for value on lettuce.)

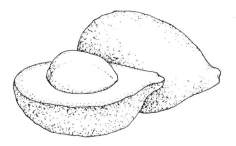

WHIPPED TOPPING
Yield: 10 servings

EACH SERVING Amount: ¼ cup		
Exchanges: Free	**Calories:** 11	**Fat:** Tr.
	Carbo: 2 gm	**Fiber:** 0 gm
Chol: Tr.	**Protein:** 1 gm	**Sodium:** 15 mg

INGREDIENTS:

¼ cup ice water
¼ cup instant nonfat dry
   milk powder

1 tablespoon lemon juice
Sugar substitute to equal ⅓
   cup sugar

STEPS IN PREPARATION:
1. Place ice water in a small bowl; gradually add milk powder, beating at high speed of an electric mixer until soft peaks form.
2. Gently fold in lemon juice and sugar substitute.
3. Cover and refrigerate until thoroughly chilled.

Note: Whipped Topping may be served on fresh fruit. (Check Exchange Lists for value on fruit.)

YOGURT-FRUIT SALAD DRESSING
Yield: 1¼ cups

EACH SERVING Amount: 2 tablespoons		
Exchanges: Free	Calories: 18	Fat: Tr.
	Carbo: 2 gm	Fiber: Tr.
Chol: 2 mg	Protein: 1 gm	Sodium: 170 mg

INGREDIENTS:
1 teaspoon grated orange
   rind
2 tablespoons unsweetened
   orange juice
2 tablespoons lemon juice

½ teaspoon dry mustard
1 teaspoon salt
¼ teaspoon paprika
1 cup plain, unsweetened
   low-fat yogurt

STEPS IN PREPARATION:
1. Combine all ingredients, except yogurt, in a small bowl, stirring until well blended; gently fold in yogurt.
2. Cover and refrigerate until thoroughly chilled.

Note: Yogurt-Fruit Salad Dressing may be served over fruit salads. (Check Exchange Lists for value on salad.)

POPPY SEED DRESSING
Yield: 1 cup

EACH SERVING Amount: 2 tablespoons		
Exchanges: ½ Vegetable	Calories: 28	Fat: 1 gm
(1 tablespoon, Free)	Carbo: 3 gm	Fiber: Tr.
Chol: 34 mg	Protein: 1 gm	Sodium: 21 mg

INGREDIENTS:
1 egg
Sugar substitute to equal ¾
   cup sugar
1 tablespoon instant minced
   onion

1 teaspoon Dijon mustard
½ cup commercial low-
   calorie Italian dressing
½ teaspoon poppy seeds
½ teaspoon sesame seeds

STEPS IN PREPARATION:
1. Combine egg, sugar substitute, onion, and mustard in container of an electric blender; cover and process until mixture is smooth.
2. With blender running, add Italian dressing in a slow steady stream, processing until blended. Stir in poppy seeds and sesame seeds.
3. Cover and refrigerate until thoroughly chilled.

Note: Poppy Seed Dressing may be served over fruit salads. (Check Exchange Lists for value on salad.)

THOUSAND ISLAND DRESSING
Yield: ¾ cup

EACH SERVING Amount: 2 tablespoons		
Exchanges: ½ Fat	**Calories:** 34	**Fat:** 2 gm
(1 tablespoon, Free)	**Carbo:** 3 gm	**Fiber:** Tr.
Chol: 8 mg	**Protein:** 1 gm	**Sodium:** 82 mg

INGREDIENTS:

¼ cup plain, unsweetened low-fat yogurt
¼ cup nonfat buttermilk
1 tablespoon low-calorie mayonnaise substitute
1 tablespoon chopped dill pickle

1 tablespoon low-calorie catsup
1 teaspoon chopped fresh parsley
⅛ teaspoon seasoned salt

STEPS IN PREPARATION:
1. Combine yogurt, buttermilk, and mayonnaise substitute in a small bowl, stirring until blended. Stir in pickle, catsup, parsley, and seasoned salt.
2. Cover and refrigerate until thoroughly chilled.

Note: Thousand Island Dressing may be served over vegetable salads. (Check Exchange Lists for value on salad.)

ITALIAN DRESSING
Yield: ¾ cup

EACH SERVING Amount: 2 tablespoons		
Exchanges: Free	**Calories:** 25	**Fat:** 1 gm
	Carbo: 1 gm	**Fiber:** Tr.
Chol: 1 mg	**Protein:** Tr.	**Sodium:** 55 mg

INGREDIENTS:
¼ cup plus 2 tablespoons
    water
¼ cup vinegar
2 tablespoons chopped fresh
    parsley
1 tablespoon plus 1
    teaspoon grated
    Parmesan cheese

2 tablespoons vegetable oil
2 teaspoons dry pectin
¼ teaspoon salt
¼ teaspoon pepper
¼ teaspoon dried whole
    Italian seasoning
1 large clove garlic, peeled

STEPS IN PREPARATION:
1. Combine all ingredients, except garlic, in a jar. Cover tightly, and shake vigorously.
2. Press a wooden pick through garlic clove; add to dressing mixture. Cover and refrigerate until thoroughly chilled.
3. To serve, remove and discard garlic. Cover and shake dressing well.

Note: Italian Dressing may be served over vegetable salads. (Check Exchange Lists for value on salad.)

NUTRIENT NEWS: The fat level in your favorite salad dressing recipe can easily be reduced. Just replace at least two-thirds of the oil called for in your dressing recipe with pureed cucumber or plain, unsweetened low-fat yogurt.

FRENCH DRESSING
Yield: 1 cup

EACH SERVING Amount: 2 tablespoons

Exchanges: 1 Fat	**Calories:** 44	**Fat:** 3 gm
(1 tablespoon, Free)	**Carbo:** 4 gm	**Fiber:** Tr.
Chol: 0 mg	**Protein:** Tr.	**Sodium:** 20 mg

INGREDIENTS:
3 tablespoons vegetable oil
¾ teaspoon salt
½ teaspoon dry mustard
⅛ teaspoon paprika

¼ teaspoon hot sauce
1 cup unsweetened
   grapefruit juice, divided
2 teaspoons cornstarch

STEPS IN PREPARATION:
1. Combine vegetable oil, salt, dry mustard, paprika, and hot sauce in a small bowl; stir until oil mixture is well blended. Set aside.
2. Combine ½ cup grapefruit juice and cornstarch in a small saucepan, stirring until blended. Cook over medium heat, stirring constantly, until mixture is thickened and bubbly. Remove from heat.
3. Add cornstarch mixture to oil mixture in bowl, and beat at medium speed of an electric mixer until smooth. Add remaining ½ cup grapefruit juice, and beat until dressing mixture is well blended.
4. Cover and refrigerate until thoroughly chilled.

Note: French Dressing may be served over vegetable salads. (Check Exchange Lists for value on salad.)

CUCUMBER DRESSING
Yield: 1 cup

EACH SERVING Amount: 2 tablespoons

Exchanges: Free	**Calories:** 15	**Fat:** Tr.
	Carbo: 2 gm	**Fiber:** Tr.
Chol: 2 mg	**Protein:** 1 gm	**Sodium:** 160 mg

INGREDIENTS:

1 small cucumber, peeled
½ teaspoon salt
½ cup plain, unsweetened
   low-fat yogurt
1 tablespoon low-calorie
   mayonnaise substitute

¼ teaspoon lemon juice
1 tablespoon chopped fresh
   parsley
1 green onion, chopped
¼ teaspoon dried whole
   dillweed

STEPS IN PREPARATION:

1. Shred cucumber. Spread on a clean towel. Sprinkle with salt. Let stand at room temperature 30 minutes. Squeeze excess moisture from cucumber.
2. Combine yogurt, mayonnaise substitute, and lemon juice in a small bowl, stirring to blend. Stir in drained cucumber, parsley, green onion, and dillweed.
3. Cover and refrigerate until thoroughly chilled. Stir well before serving.

Note: Cucumber Dressing may be served over vegetable salads. (Check Exchange Lists for value on salad.)

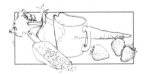

Recipes

Desserts

APPLE PUDDING
Yield: 6 servings

EACH SERVING Amount: 1 square

Exchanges: 1½ Starch	**Calories:** 157	**Fat:** 5 gm
1 Fat	**Carbo:** 24 gm	**Fiber:** 1 gm
Chol: 51 mg	**Protein:** 4 gm	**Sodium:** 330 mg

INGREDIENTS:

3 medium-size cooking apples, peeled and sliced
Vegetable cooking spray
1 cup all-purpose flour
1 teaspoon baking powder
¼ teaspoon salt
⅓ cup reduced-calorie margarine

Sugar substitute to equal ⅓ cup sugar
½ teaspoon grated lemon rind
½ teaspoon vanilla extract
1 egg
½ cup skim milk

STEPS IN PREPARATION:

1. Arrange apple slices in bottom of an 8-inch square baking pan coated with cooking spray. Set aside.
2. Combine flour, baking powder, and salt, stirring until blended. Set aside.
3. Combine margarine, sugar substitute, rind, and vanilla in a medium bowl; beat at medium speed of an electric mixer until well blended. Add egg; beat until fluffy.
4. Add flour mixture to creamed mixture alternately with milk, beginning and ending with flour mixture.
5. Spoon batter into prepared pan, and bake at 375° for 40 to 45 minutes or until a wooden pick inserted in center comes out clean. Cut into 6 squares, and serve hot.

OLD-FASHIONED BREAD PUDDING
Yield: 8 servings

EACH SERVING Amount: ½ cup		
Exchanges: 1 Starch	**Calories:** 139	**Fat:** 4 gm
1 Fat	**Carbo:** 19 gm	**Fiber:** Tr.
½ Skim Milk	**Protein:** 7 gm	**Sodium:** 160 mg
Chol: 138 mg		

INGREDIENTS:
6 slices day-old white bread, crust removed

2 tablespoons reduced-calorie margarine, melted

Sugar substitute to equal ¾ cup sugar, divided

1 teaspoon ground cinnamon

½ cup seedless raisins

Vegetable cooking spray

4 eggs, beaten

2 cups skim milk

1 teaspoon vanilla extract

STEPS IN PREPARATION:
1. Brush bread lightly with melted margarine; sprinkle with 1 teaspoon sugar substitute and cinnamon.
2. Quarter each bread slice. Layer with raisins in a 1½-quart casserole dish coated with cooking spray. Set dish aside.
3. Combine eggs, milk, vanilla, and remaining 2 teaspoons sugar substitute; pour over bread and raisins in dish.
4. Place dish in a pan containing 1 inch of hot water. Bake at 350° for 55 minutes to 1 hour or until a knife inserted in center comes out clean. Serve warm, or cover and refrigerate until thoroughly chilled.

HELPFUL HINT: To enhance the flavor of water-packed fruit, drain the fruit, reserving the liquid. Add 1 to 2 teaspoons lemon juice and sugar substitute to taste to the liquid, stirring well. Pour the liquid back over the fruit. Cover tightly, and store in the refrigerator 24 hours.

BAKED CUSTARD
Yield: 5 servings

EACH SERVING Amount: ½ cup

Exchanges: ½ Skim Milk
½ Fat
Chol: 56 mg

Calories: 66
Carbo: 5 gm
Protein: 6 gm

Fat: 2 gm
Fiber: 0 gm
Sodium: 78 mg

INGREDIENTS:
2 eggs
2 cups skim milk

Liquid sugar substitute to
equal ⅓ cup sugar
2 teaspoons vanilla extract

STEPS IN PREPARATION:
1. Lightly beat eggs in a small bowl; add remaining ingredients, and beat well.
2. Pour mixture into five 6-ounce custard cups, and place cups in a pan containing 1 inch of hot water.
3. Bake at 350° for 45 minutes or until a knife inserted in center comes out clean. Cover and chill thoroughly.

PEACH CRUMB BAKE
Yield: 4 servings

EACH SERVING Amount: ½ cup

Exchanges: 1 Fruit
½ Fat
Chol: 0 mg

Calories: 78
Carbo: 15 gm
Protein: 1 gm

Fat: 2 gm
Fiber: 1 gm
Sodium: 27 mg

INGREDIENTS:
2 cups sliced fresh peaches
Vegetable cooking spray
⅓ cup graham cracker
crumbs

½ teaspoon ground
cinnamon
⅛ teaspoon ground nutmeg
2 teaspoons reduced-calorie
margarine, melted

STEPS IN PREPARATION:
1. Layer sliced peaches in bottom of an 8-inch square baking dish coated with vegetable cooking spray. Combine graham cracker crumbs, cinnamon, and nutmeg in a small bowl, stirring well. Add margarine, and stir until well combined.
2. Sprinkle graham cracker crumb mixture over peaches, and bake at 350° for 30 minutes. Serve warm.

SUGARLESS APPLE DESSERT
Yield: 5 servings

EACH SERVING Amount: ½ cup		
Exchanges: 1½ Starch	**Calories:** 121	**Fat:** 2 gm
	Carbo: 25 gm	**Fiber:** 1 gm
Chol: 0 mg	**Protein:** 4 gm	**Sodium:** 35 mg

INGREDIENTS:
3 envelopes unflavored gelatin
1 (12-ounce) can unsweetened frozen apple juice concentrate, diluted with 1 can water
½ teaspoon ground cinnamon
½ teaspoon ground nutmeg
5 cups peeled, sliced apples
1 tablespoon reduced-calorie margarine

STEPS IN PREPARATION:
1. Combine gelatin, diluted apple juice concentrate, cinnamon, and nutmeg in a large skillet, stirring well; let stand 1 minute. Cook over low heat 1 minute or until gelatin dissolves. Add apples. Cover and continue to cook over low heat 15 to 20 minutes or until tender.
2. Stir apples gently, and baste with pan juice several times during cooking process.
3. Add margarine; stir gently until margarine melts. Remove from heat.
4. Cover and refrigerate until thoroughly chilled. Spoon mixture into dessert dishes to serve.

EASY BLUEBERRY COBBLER
Yield: 6 servings

EACH SERVING Amount: ½ cup

Exchanges: 1 Starch	Calories: 168	Fat: 6 gm
1 Fruit	Carbo: 27 gm	Fiber: 1 gm
1 Fat	Protein: 3 gm	Sodium: 114 mg
Chol: 50 mg		

INGREDIENTS:
3 cups fresh blueberries
Vegetable cooking spray
1 tablespoon lemon juice
1 egg, beaten
1 cup all-purpose flour

Sugar substitute to equal 1½
  cups sugar
¼ cup plus 2 tablespoons
  reduced-calorie
  margarine, melted

STEPS IN PREPARATION:
1. Place blueberries in bottom of a 10- x 6- x 2-inch baking dish coated with cooking spray; sprinkle with lemon juice.
2. Combine egg, flour, and sugar substitute; stir until mixture resembles coarse meal. Sprinkle over blueberries.
3. Drizzle melted margarine over top. Bake at 375° for 30 minutes. Serve warm.

GINGER FRUIT
Yield: 8 servings

EACH SERVING Amount: ¾ cup

Exchanges: 1 Fruit	Calories: 75	Fat: Tr.
	Carbo: 19 gm	Fiber: 1 gm
Chol: 0 mg	Protein: 1 gm	Sodium: 1 mg

INGREDIENTS:
2 medium apples, unpeeled
  and sliced
2 medium-size oranges
  peeled, seeded, and
  sectioned

2 medium bananas, sliced
½ cup unsweetened orange
  juice
1 teaspoon ground ginger

STEPS IN PREPARATION:
1. Combine apples, oranges, and bananas in a medium bowl. Combine orange juice and ginger, stirring until blended.
2. Pour orange juice mixture over fruit, and toss lightly to coat. Cover and refrigerate 2 hours.

SPICED FRUIT
Yield: 8 servings

EACH SERVING Amount: ¾ cup		
Exchanges: 1 Fruit	**Calories:** 60	**Fat:** Tr.
	Carbo: 15 gm	**Fiber:** 1 gm
Chol: 0 mg	**Protein:** Tr.	**Sodium:** 3 mg

INGREDIENTS:
1 medium-size orange
1 (15¼-ounce) can unsweetened pineapple chunks, undrained
2 (16-ounce) cans unsweetened pear halves, drained

1 (16-ounce) can unsweetened apricot halves, drained
2 (2-inch) sticks cinnamon
6 whole cloves

STEPS IN PREPARATION:
1. Peel orange, reserving rind. Section orange, and remove seeds. Drain pineapple, reserving juice.
2. Combine orange sections, pineapple chunks, pear halves, and apricot halves in a large bowl; set aside.
3. Combine orange rind, pineapple juice, cinnamon, and cloves in a small saucepan, stirring well. Bring to a boil; reduce heat, and simmer 5 minutes. Remove from heat.
4. Strain mixture, discarding rind and whole spices. Pour juice over fruit, tossing gently to combine. Cover and refrigerate until thoroughly chilled.

SPICED PEACH DESSERT
Yield: 3 servings

EACH SERVING Amount: ½ cup

Exchanges: 1 Fruit	**Calories:** 49	**Fat:** Tr.
	Carbo: 12 gm	**Fiber:** 1 gm
Chol: 0 mg	**Protein:** Tr.	**Sodium:** 5 mg

INGREDIENTS:

1 (16-ounce) can
    unsweetened peach
    halves, undrained
½ teaspoon cornstarch
⅛ teaspoon ground
    cinnamon

⅛ teaspoon ground nutmeg
⅛ teaspoon ground cloves
⅛ teaspoon grated orange
    rind

STEPS IN PREPARATION:

1. Drain peaches, reserving juice; set peaches aside.
2. Combine cornstarch and spices in a medium saucepan; stir in peach juice and rind.
3. Add peaches to mixture in saucepan; bring to a boil, stirring constantly. Reduce heat, and simmer 2 minutes, stirring occasionally.
4. Remove from heat, and serve warm.

CALORIE CURB: You don't have to starve yourself or suffer from tasteless food to eat fewer calories. You can cut calories and still enjoy good taste by making smart substitutions. For example, for a cup of sliced peaches canned in syrup (200 calories), substitute a cup of sliced peaches canned in water (75 calories).

TASTY PINEAPPLE CAKE
Yield: 12 servings

EACH SERVING Amount: 1 slice

Exchanges: 1 Starch	**Calories:** 129	**Fat:** 5 gm
1 Fat	**Carbo:** 17 gm	**Fiber:** Tr.
Chol: 46 mg	**Protein:** 3 gm	**Sodium:** 341 mg

INGREDIENTS:
½ cup reduced-calorie
  margarine
Sugar substitute to equal 2¼
  cups sugar, divided
2 eggs
1½ cups all-purpose flour
1 teaspoon baking powder
½ teaspoon baking soda

¼ teaspoon salt
½ cup skim milk
4 slices unsweetened
  canned pineapple,
  drained
Vegetable cooking spray
½ cup unsweetened
  pineapple juice

STEPS IN PREPARATION:
1. Cream margarine and 2 tablespoons sugar substitute until light and fluffy. Add eggs, one at a time, beating well at medium speed of an electric mixer.
2. Combine flour, baking powder, soda, and salt. Add to creamed mixture alternately with milk, beginning and ending with flour mixture. Beat at low speed after each addition. Cut pineapple into ½-inch pieces, and gently fold into batter.
3. Spoon batter into a 6-cup Bundt pan or heavy ring mold coated with cooking spray. Bake at 350° for 45 to 50 minutes or until a wooden pick inserted in center comes out clean.
4. Combine pineapple juice and remaining 1 tablespoon sugar substitute, stirring until sugar substitute dissolves. Remove cake from oven, and immediately pour juice mixture over cake; let stand 5 minutes. Remove cake from pan, and cool completely on a wire rack.

ORANGE STREUSEL CAKE

Yield: 12 servings

EACH SERVING Amount: 1 slice		
Exchanges: 1½ Starch	**Calories:** 133	**Fat:** 4 gm
1 Fat	**Carbo:** 21 gm	**Fiber:** Tr.
Chol: 24 mg	**Protein:** 4 gm	**Sodium:** 156 mg

INGREDIENTS: .

1 package dry yeast
Sugar substitute to equal ⅓ cup sugar, divided
½ cup warm water (105° to 115°)
1 egg
2¾ cups all-purpose flour, divided
2 tablespoons reduced-calorie margarine, melted

2 tablespoons low-calorie orange marmalade
½ teaspoon salt
Vegetable cooking spray
¼ cup reduced-calorie margarine, melted
1 tablespoon grated orange rind
1 tablespoon unsweetened orange juice

STEPS IN PREPARATION:

1. Dissolve yeast and ¼ teaspoon sugar substitute in warm water in a large bowl; let stand 5 minutes. Add egg, beating well at medium speed of an electric mixer.
2. Add 1 cup flour, 2 tablespoons melted margarine, marmalade, and salt. Beat until smooth. Gradually add 1¼ cups flour to make a soft dough, stirring until smooth.
3. Turn dough out onto a lightly floured surface, and knead until smooth and elastic (8 to 10 minutes). Place dough in a bowl coated with cooking spray, turning to grease top.
4. Cover and let rise in a warm place (85°), free from drafts, 50 minutes or until doubled in bulk. Punch dough down. Press dough evenly into a 9-inch round or square baking pan coated with cooking spray.
5. Combine remaining 1 teaspoon sugar substitute, remaining ½ cup flour, ¼ cup melted margarine, orange rind, and orange juice; stir well, and sprinkle over dough. Cover and

let rise in a warm place (85°), free from drafts, 25 minutes or until doubled in bulk.

6. Bake at 375° for 25 to 30 minutes or until a wooden pick inserted in center comes out clean. Serve warm.

SUNSHINE ORANGE CAKE
Yield: 9 servings

EACH SERVING Amount: 1 square		
Exchanges: 1 Starch	**Calories:** 118	**Fat:** 3 gm
1 Fat	**Carbo:** 19 gm	**Fiber:** Tr.
Chol: 30 mg	**Protein:** 3 gm	**Sodium:** 257 mg

INGREDIENTS:

⅓ cup reduced-calorie margarine, melted

Brown sugar substitute to equal ¼ cup brown sugar

Sugar substitute to equal ¼ cup sugar

1 egg

1¼ cups all-purpose flour

2 teaspoons baking powder

½ teaspoon baking soda

¼ teaspoon ground cinnamon

⅓ cup raisins

⅔ cup unsweetened orange juice

Vegetable cooking spray

STEPS IN PREPARATION:

1. Combine margarine, sugar substitutes, and egg; beat at high speed of an electric mixer 2 minutes.
2. Combine flour, baking powder, soda, and cinnamon, stirring to blend. Stir in raisins.
3. Add flour mixture to creamed mixture alternately with orange juice, beginning and ending with flour mixture. Beat at low speed of an electric mixer after each addition.
4. Spoon batter into an 8-inch square baking pan coated with cooking spray. Bake at 350° for 25 to 30 minutes or until a wooden pick inserted in center comes out clean. Cut into squares to serve.

RAISIN CAKE
Yield: 24 slices

EACH SERVING Amount: 1 slice

Exchanges: 1½ Starch	**Calories:** 170	**Fat:** 4 gm
1 Fat	**Carbo:** 24 gm	**Fiber:** Tr.
Chol: 22 mg	**Protein:** 3 gm	**Sodium:** 222 mg

INGREDIENTS:

2 cups water
1 cup reduced-calorie
   margarine
1 (15-ounce) package raisins
Sugar substitute to equal 3
   cups sugar
2 teaspoons baking soda
¼ cup warm water

2 eggs, beaten
4½ cups all-purpose flour
1 teaspoon ground cloves
1 teaspoon ground allspice
1 teaspoon ground
   cinnamon
½ teaspoon baking powder
Vegetable cooking spray

STEPS IN PREPARATION:

1. Bring 2 cups water to a boil in a large saucepan; stir in margarine and raisins, and boil, uncovered, 5 minutes. Remove from heat, and cool raisin mixture to lukewarm. Stir in sugar substitute.
2. Dissolve soda in ¼ cup warm water; add to raisin mixture, stirring well. Stir in eggs.
3. Combine flour, cloves, allspice, cinnamon, and baking powder; gradually add to raisin mixture, stirring after each addition.
4. Spoon batter into a 10-inch Bundt pan coated with vegetable cooking spray. Bake at 375° for 50 minutes to 1 hour or until a wooden pick inserted in center comes out clean. Cool cake in Bundt pan 10 minutes. Remove from pan; let cool on a wire rack.

APPLESAUCE-SPICE CAKE
Yield: 28 slices

EACH SERVING Amount: 1 slice		
Exchanges: 2 Fat	**Calories:** 165	**Fat:** 8 gm
1 Starch	**Carbo:** 20 gm	**Fiber:** Tr.
½ Fruit	**Protein:** 2 gm	**Sodium:** 26 mg
Chol: 29 mg		

INGREDIENTS:

3 cups water, divided
1¼ cups raisins
2½ cups unsweetened applesauce
3 eggs, beaten
Sugar substitute to equal 1½ cups sugar

1 cup vegetable oil
3 cups self-rising flour
3 tablespoons ground cinnamon
¼ teaspoon baking soda
2 tablespoons vanilla extract
Vegetable cooking spray

STEPS IN PREPARATION:

1. Combine 2½ cups water and raisins in a small Dutch oven; bring to a boil. Boil until water evaporates or is absorbed by raisins. Remove from heat.
2. Add applesauce, eggs, sugar substitute, oil, and remaining ½ cup water. Stir until well combined.
3. Sift together flour, cinnamon, and soda; gradually add to applesauce mixture with vanilla, stirring after each addition.
4. Spoon batter into a 10-inch Bundt pan coated with cooking spray. Bake at 350° for 40 to 45 minutes or until a wooden pick inserted in center comes out clean. Cool in pan 10 minutes; remove from pan, and cool on a wire rack.

CALORIE CURB: Try your hand at creative cooking to cut calories and add interest. Take your favorite angel food cake recipe and try a new extract or flavoring. Substitute a favorite fresh fruit for calorie-laden sauces or toppings.

FROZEN LEMON DESSERT
Yield: 9 servings

EACH SERVING Amount: 1 square

Exchanges: ½ Skim Milk	**Calories:** 42	**Fat:** 1 gm
	Carbo: 5 gm	**Fiber:** Tr.
Chol: 59 mg	**Protein:** 3 gm	**Sodium:** 52 mg

INGREDIENTS:

1 cup evaporated skim milk
2 eggs, separated
1 teaspoon grated lemon
   rind

½ cup lemon juice, divided
Sugar substitute to equal ⅓
   cup sugar
¼ cup graham cracker
   crumbs

STEPS IN PREPARATION:

1. Place evaporated skim milk in a 9-inch square baking pan; cover and freeze 1½ hours or until slushy.
2. Combine egg yolks, lemon rind, ¼ cup lemon juice, and sugar substitute; beat at medium speed of an electric mixer until smooth. Set aside.
3. Combine partially frozen milk and egg whites in a large chilled bowl; beat with chilled beaters until foamy. Add remaining ¼ cup lemon juice; beat until stiff peaks form. Gently fold yolk mixture into milk mixture.
4. Pour mixture into baking pan; sprinkle with graham cracker crumbs. Cover and freeze 4 hours or until firm. Cut into squares to serve.

EXERCISE BREAK: Don't overlook walking when planning an exercise program for yourself. It's an easy way to get up and get started, and it's just plain good for you. Start out by walking a few blocks and gradually work up to a mile or two. Even a leisurely stroll four or five times a week will reap health benefits.

CHOCOLATE AND FRUIT PARFAITS
Yield: 6 servings

EACH SERVING Amount: 1 parfait		
Exchanges: 1 Fruit	**Calories:** 112	**Fat:** 1 gm
½ Skim Milk	**Carbo:** 22 gm	**Fiber:** 1 gm
Chol: 2 mg	**Protein:** 5 gm	**Sodium:** 68 mg

INGREDIENTS:
1 cup cold water
2 tablespoons cocoa
Sugar substitute to equal ½ cup plus 2 tablespoons sugar, divided

1 cup instant nonfat dry milk powder
2 cups sliced fresh strawberries
2 bananas, sliced

STEPS IN PREPARATION:
1. Combine water and cocoa in a small saucepan; bring to a boil, stirring constantly with a wire whisk to dissolve cocoa. Remove from heat, and let cool. Stir in 1½ teaspoons sugar substitute.
2. Cover and refrigerate until mixture is thoroughly chilled. Add milk powder, and beat at high speed of an electric mixer until mixture is thick and fluffy. Cover and refrigerate until thoroughly chilled.
3. Sprinkle remaining 1 teaspoon sugar substitute over strawberries; let stand at room temperature 20 minutes. Divide half of sliced strawberries equally among 6 parfait glasses. Set remaining strawberries aside.
4. Spoon ⅓ cup chilled cocoa mixture over strawberries in parfait glasses; divide banana slices evenly over top.
5. Top each parfait with remaining strawberries.

FRUIT PARFAITS
Yield: 6 servings

EACH SERVING Amount: ½ cup		
Exchanges: 1 Starch	Calories: 87	Fat: 2 gm
	Carbo: 17 gm	Fiber: 1 gm
Chol: 1 mg	Protein: 2 gm	Sodium: 18 mg

INGREDIENTS:

½ cup Whipped Topping
(see page 181)
¼ cup unsweetened grated
coconut
2 tablespoons frozen orange
juice concentrate,
thawed and undiluted

1 large orange, peeled,
seeded, and sectioned
1 large banana, sliced
1 cup cubed fresh pineapple

STEPS IN PREPARATION:
1. Combine first 3 ingredients, stirring well. Combine orange, banana, and pineapple; toss lightly.
2. Spoon alternate layers of fruit mixture and orange juice mixture into 6 parfait glasses. Cover and chill thoroughly.

STRAWBERRY MOUSSE
Yield: 6 servings

EACH SERVING Amount: ½ cup		
Exchanges: ½ Skim Milk	Calories: 45	Fat: Tr.
	Carbo: 7 gm	Fiber: Tr.
Chol: 1 mg	Protein: 4 gm	Sodium: 53 mg

INGREDIENTS:

1 (0.3-ounce) package
sugar-free, strawberry-
flavored gelatin
½ cup water

1½ cups sliced fresh
strawberries
⅔ cup instant nonfat dry
milk powder
6 ice cubes

STEPS IN PREPARATION:
1. Combine gelatin and water in small saucepan, stirring well; let stand 1 minute. Cook over low heat 1 minute or until gelatin dissolves, stirring constantly.
2. Combine gelatin mixture, strawberries, and milk powder in container of an electric blender; cover and process until smooth. Uncover and add ice cubes, one at a time, processing until blended.
3. Spoon mixture into 6 parfait glasses. Cover and refrigerate until thoroughly chilled.

ORANGE DELIGHT
Yield: 8 servings

EACH SERVING Amount: ¾ cup		
Exchanges: 1 Skim Milk	**Calories:** 78	**Fat:** Tr.
	Carbo: 10 gm	**Fiber:** Tr.
Chol: 3 mg	**Protein:** 7 gm	**Sodium:** 137 mg

INGREDIENTS:
2 cups low-fat cottage cheese

2 cups unsweetened crushed pineapple, well drained

1 (0.3-ounce) package sugar-free, orange-flavored gelatin

2 cups Whipped Topping (see page 181)

Sliced fresh strawberries (optional)

Fresh mint sprigs (optional)

STEPS IN PREPARATION:
1. Gently fold cottage cheese, crushed pineapple, and dry gelatin into Whipped Topping. Cover and refrigerate until thoroughly chilled.
2. Spoon into dessert dishes, and, if desired, garnish each serving with strawberry slices and mint sprigs. (Check Exchange Lists for value on strawberries.)

PINEAPPLE DESSERT
Yield: 6 servings

EACH SERVING Amount: ½ cup

Exchanges: 1 Fruit

Chol: 1 mg

Calories: 78
Carbo: 17 gm
Protein: 4 gm

Fat: Tr.
Fiber: Tr.
Sodium: 34 mg

INGREDIENTS:

1 (15¼-ounce) can unsweetened crushed pineapple, undrained

1 envelope unflavored gelatin

¼ teaspoon vanilla extract

½ cup instant nonfat dry milk powder

⅓ cup ice water

2 tablespoons lemon juice

Sugar substitute to equal 2 teaspoons sugar

STEPS IN PREPARATION:

1. Drain pineapple, reserving liquid. Set crushed pineapple aside. Add water to pineapple liquid to yield 1 cup.
2. Combine liquid mixture and gelatin in a small saucepan, stirring well; let stand 1 minute. Cook over low heat 1 minute or until gelatin dissolves, stirring constantly. Remove from heat, and stir in crushed pineapple and vanilla. Refrigerate until mixture reaches the consistency of unbeaten egg white.
3. Combine dry milk powder and ice water in a medium bowl; beat at medium speed of an electric mixer until foamy. Add lemon juice; continue to beat 3 to 4 minutes or until soft peaks form, gradually adding sugar substitute.
4. Fold gelatin mixture into whipped milk mixture. Spoon into six 6-ounce custard cups or dessert dishes. Cover and refrigerate until thoroughly chilled.

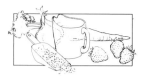

Recipes

Snacks

STRAWBERRY SPREAD
Yield: 32 servings

EACH SERVING Amount: 1 tablespoon

Exchanges: Free	**Calories:** 11	**Fat:** Tr.
	Carbo: 3 gm	**Fiber:** Tr.
Chol: 0 mg	**Protein:** Tr.	**Sodium:** 3 mg

INGREDIENTS:
1 quart fresh strawberries, washed, hulled, and coarsely chopped
¾ cup cold water, divided
2 tablespoons lemon juice
¼ teaspoon ground cinnamon
3 tablespoons cornstarch
Sugar substitute to equal 1 cup sugar

STEPS IN PREPARATION:
1. Combine strawberries, ½ cup water, lemon juice, and cinnamon in a small Dutch oven, stirring well; bring mixture to a boil.
2. Dissolve cornstarch in remaining ¼ cup water, and stir into boiling mixture. Reduce heat, and simmer 2 to 3 minutes or until mixture thickens, stirring occasionally.
3. Remove from heat, and cool. Stir in sugar substitute.

Note: Strawberry Spread may be served over graham crackers or toast. (Check Exchange Lists for values on graham crackers or toast.)

CALORIE CURB: If you're making changes in your lifestyle to help you control weight or diabetes, make those changes slowly and one at a time. For instance, if you want to eliminate the fat in whole milk from your diet, start by mixing your whole milk with 2% milk. Gradually phase out the whole milk, then try mixing your 2% milk with skim. Eventually you'll be drinking only skim milk with 0.4% fat.

TOFU SANDWICH SPREAD
Yield: 12 servings

EACH SERVING Amount: 2 tablespoons		
Exchanges: Free	**Calories:** 20	**Fat:** 1 gm
	Carbo: 1 gm	**Fiber:** Tr.
Chol: 1 mg	**Protein:** 1 gm	**Sodium:** 14 mg

INGREDIENTS:

1 (8-ounce) package tofu, drained, rinsed, and mashed

2 tablespoons low-calorie mayonnaise substitute

½ teaspoon celery salt

¼ teaspoon ground turmeric

¼ teaspoon dry mustard

¼ teaspoon dried whole dillweed

2 green onions, sliced

1 stalk celery, finely chopped

1 tablespoon chopped fresh parsley

1 tablespoon finely chopped dill pickle

STEPS IN PREPARATION:

1. Combine mashed tofu, mayonnaise substitute, celery salt, turmeric, mustard, and dillweed in a medium bowl, stirring until blended.
2. Add green onions and remaining ingredients to tofu mixture, stirring gently. Cover and store in refrigerator until ready to serve.

Note: Tofu Sandwich Spread may be served on whole wheat bread. (Check Exchange Lists for value on bread.)

NUTRIENT NEWS: Tofu is a low-fat, high-protein, cholesterol-free soy food that can be substituted for ricotta and cottage cheese in recipes to cut even more dairy calories. Since tofu is milder in flavor, it may be necessary to add additional seasoning to bring out the flavor of the recipe.

PIMIENTO CHEESE
Yield: 8 servings

EACH SERVING Amount: ¼ cup

Exchanges: 1 Lean Meat	**Calories:** 48	**Fat:** 1 gm
	Carbo: 2 gm	**Fiber:** Tr.
Chol: 4 mg	**Protein:** 7 gm	**Sodium:** 306 mg

INGREDIENTS:
- 1 cup (4 ounces) shredded low-fat process American cheese
- 1 cup low-fat cottage cheese
- 2 (4-ounce) jars diced pimiento, drained

STEPS IN PREPARATION:
1. Position knife blade in food processor bowl; add all ingredients. Top with cover; pulse several times until coarsely blended.
2. Cover and store in refrigerator until ready to serve.

Note: Pimiento Cheese may be served as a spread on whole wheat bread. (Check Exchange Lists for value on bread.)

PARMESAN-SESAME STICKS
Yield: 8 dozen sticks

EACH SERVING Amount: 4 sticks

Exchanges: 1 Vegetable	**Calories:** 40	**Fat:** 2 gm
	Carbo: 4 gm	**Fiber:** Tr.
Chol: Tr.	**Protein:** 1 gm	**Sodium:** 87 mg

INGREDIENTS:
- 12 slices white bread, crust removed
- ¼ cup reduced-calorie margarine, melted
- ¼ cup grated Parmesan cheese
- 2 tablespoons sesame seeds

STEPS IN PREPARATION:
1. Cut each slice of bread into 8 sticks, and arrange on ungreased baking sheets.
2. Brush breadsticks lightly with margarine. Sprinkle evenly with Parmesan cheese and sesame seeds.
3. Bake at 350° for 10 to 15 minutes or until golden brown. Serve immediately.

COTTAGE CHEESE-VEGETABLE DUNK
Yield: 28 servings

EACH SERVING Amount: 2 tablespoons		
Exchanges: Free	**Calories:** 22	**Fat:** Tr.
	Carbo: 1 gm	**Fiber:** Tr.
Chol: 1 mg	**Protein:** 3 gm	**Sodium:** 134 mg

INGREDIENTS:
2 (8-ounce) cartons low-fat cottage cheese

1 cup (4 ounces) shredded low-fat process American cheese

3 tablespoons plain, unsweetened low-fat yogurt

2 tablespoons prepared horseradish

½ teaspoon pepper

¼ teaspoon salt

2 tablespoons chopped green pepper

2 tablespoons minced onion

STEPS IN PREPARATION:
1. Combine cottage cheese, American cheese, yogurt, horseradish, pepper, and salt, in a medium bowl, stirring well. Gently fold in green pepper and onion.
2. Cover and store in refrigerator until ready to serve.

Note: Serve Cottage Cheese-Vegetable Dunk with raw vegetables. (Check Exchange Lists for values on raw vegetables.)

CRUNCHY NOODLE JUMBLE
Yield: 8 servings

EACH SERVING Amount: ¼ cup

Exchanges: 1 Fat	Calories: 75	Fat: 5 gm
½ Starch	Carbo: 7 gm	Fiber: Tr.
Chol: 1 mg	Protein: 2 gm	Sodium: 174 mg

INGREDIENTS:
1 (3-ounce) can chow mein
    noodles
½ teaspoon chili powder
¼ teaspoon garlic salt
¼ teaspoon dry mustard

2 tablespoons
    reduced-calorie
    margarine, melted
1 tablespoon sesame seeds
1 tablespoon reduced-
    sodium soy sauce

STEPS IN PREPARATION:
1. Combine all ingredients in a 13- x 9- x 2-inch baking pan, tossing lightly to coat. Bake at 350° for 15 to 20 minutes, stirring once during baking time.
2. Remove from oven, and serve hot.

FRUITY GELATIN SNACK
Yield: 8 servings

EACH SERVING Amount: ½ cup

Exchanges: Free	Calories: 24	Fat: Tr.
	Carbo: 0 gm	Fiber: 0 gm
Chol: 0 mg	Protein: 5 gm	Sodium: 78 mg

INGREDIENTS:
4 envelopes unflavored
    gelatin
3 (0.3-ounce) packages
    sugar-free, fruit-flavored
    gelatin

4 cups boiling water
Vegetable cooking spray

1. Combine unflavored gelatin and fruit-flavored gelatin in a medium bowl. Add boiling water, and stir until gelatin dissolves.
2. Pour gelatin mixture into an 8-inch square baking pan coated with cooking spray. Cover and refrigerate until firm.
3. Cut into 1-inch squares to serve.

FRUIT AND RUM YOGURT

Yield: 4 servings

EACH SERVING Amount: ½ cup		
Exchanges: 1 Milk	**Calories:** 77	**Fat:** 1 gm
	Carbo: 10 gm	**Fiber:** Tr.
Chol: 6 mg	**Protein:** 6 gm	**Sodium:** 79 mg

INGREDIENTS:

1½ cups plain, unsweetened low-fat yogurt

¼ cup evaporated skim milk

2 teaspoons rum extract

⅓ cup canned, water-packed fruit cocktail, drained

STEPS IN PREPARATION:

1. Combine yogurt, evaporated skim milk, and rum extract in a medium bowl, stirring well. Gently fold in fruit cocktail.
2. Cover and refrigerate up to 2 days. Stir gently before serving in individual dessert dishes.

MINI-SNACK: Prepare ½ cup broccoli flowerets, ½ cup cauliflowerets, and 1 carrot, cut into strips; then serve with ¼ cup plain low-fat yogurt that has been combined with chopped fresh dillweed to taste. Yield: 3 mini-snacks with 30 calories and 1 Vegetable exchange per mini-snack.

FRUIT-YOGURT SNACK
Yield: 12 servings

EACH SERVING Amount: ⅔ cup

Exchanges: 1 Fruit	Calories: 69	Fat: Tr.
	Carbo: 16 gm	Fiber: Tr.
Chol: 1 mg	Protein: 1 gm	Sodium: 14 mg

INGREDIENTS:

1 (15¼-ounce) can water-packed pineapple chunks, drained
2 medium bananas, sliced
2 medium apples, unpeeled and cut into ½-inch cubes

½ cup unsweetened orange juice
1 (8-ounce) carton plain, unsweetened low-fat yogurt
¼ teaspoon ground ginger

STEPS IN PREPARATION:

1. Combine first 4 ingredients in a large bowl; toss gently. Cover and chill thoroughly; drain.
2. Combine yogurt and ginger, stirring to blend; pour over fruit, and toss gently to coat. Serve immediately.

FROZEN FRUIT FREEZE
Yield: 15 servings

EACH SERVING Amount: ⅓ cup

Exchanges: 1 Fruit	Calories: 54	Fat: Tr.
	Carbo: 13 gm	Fiber: Tr.
Chol: 0 mg	Protein: 1 gm	Sodium: 1 mg

INGREDIENTS:

2 cups mashed ripe bananas
1 (8-ounce) can water-packed crushed pineapple, undrained

2 cups unsweetened orange juice
2 tablespoons lemon juice

STEPS IN PREPARATION:
1. Combine all ingredients, stirring well; pour into an 8-inch square baking pan. Freeze mixture until almost firm.
2. Spoon mixture into a large bowl, and beat at medium speed of an electric mixer until smooth and creamy. Spoon mixture back into pan, and freeze until firm. Serve in individual dessert dishes.

ORANGE-BANANA POPS
Yield: 6 pops

EACH SERVING Amount: 1 pop		
Exchanges: 1 Fruit	**Calories:** 77	**Fat:** Tr.
	Carbo: 19 gm	**Fiber:** Tr.
Chol: 0 mg	**Protein:** 1 gm	**Sodium:** 2 mg

INGREDIENTS:

3 medium bananas, mashed
1 cup unsweetened orange juice
¼ cup water
1 teaspoon lime juice
Sugar substitute to equal 2 teaspoons sugar

STEPS IN PREPARATION:
1. Combine all ingredients, beating well at low speed of an electric mixer. Pour evenly into six 5-ounce paper cups.
2. Partially freeze; insert a wooden stick into center of each cup, and freeze until firm.
3. When ready to serve, let pops stand at room temperature 5 minutes; peel away cups.

SUGARLESS OATMEAL COOKIES
Yield: 2½ dozen cookies

EACH SERVING Amount: 1 cookie		
Exchanges: ½ Starch	Calories: 45	Fat: 1 gm
	Carbo: 8 gm	Fiber: Tr.
Chol: Tr.	Protein: 1 gm	Sodium: 73 mg

INGREDIENTS:

3 bananas, mashed
2 cups uncooked
   quick-cooking oats
½ cup raisins

⅓ cup reduced-calorie
   margarine, melted
¼ cup skim milk
1 teaspoon vanilla extract

STEPS IN PREPARATION:
1. Combine all ingredients, beating well. Let stand 5 minutes so that oats will absorb moisture.
2. Drop dough by heaping teaspoonfuls onto ungreased cookie sheets, and bake at 350° for 15 to 20 minutes. Let stand 1 minute on cookie sheets; transfer to wire racks to cool completely.

ALMOND COOKIES
Yield: 22 cookies

EACH SERVING Amount: 2 cookies		
Exchanges: ½ Starch	Calories: 80	Fat: 4 gm
½ Fat	Carbo: 10 gm	Fiber: Tr.
Chol: 10 mg	Protein: 1 gm	Sodium: 61 mg

INGREDIENTS:

¼ cup plus 2 tablespoons
   reduced-calorie
   margarine
Sugar substitute to equal ¼
   cup sugar
1 egg yolk

½ teaspoon almond extract
¼ teaspoon vanilla extract
¼ teaspoon lemon extract
1 cup all-purpose flour
½ teaspoon baking powder
⅛ teaspoon salt

1. Cream margarine and sugar substitute in a medium bowl, beating at medium speed of an electric mixer until light and fluffy. Add egg yolk and flavorings; beat well.
2. Combine flour, baking powder, and salt; add to creamed mixture, beating well.
3. Shape dough into 1-inch balls; place 2 inches apart on ungreased cookie sheets. Press each with a fork to flatten.
4. Bake at 350° for 15 minutes or until edges begin to brown. Remove cookies to wire racks, and cool completely.

APPLESAUCE-RAISIN BARS
Yield: 2 dozen bars

EACH SERVING Amount: 2 bars		
Exchanges: 1 Starch	**Calories:** 81	**Fat:** 2 gm
	Carbo: 14 gm	**Fiber:** Tr.
Chol: 11 mg	**Protein:** 2 gm	**Sodium:** 57 mg

INGREDIENTS:

¼ cup reduced-calorie margarine
Brown sugar substitute to equal ⅔ cup brown sugar
1 egg
1 cup all-purpose flour

1 teaspoon baking powder
1 teaspoon apple pie spice
½ cup raisins, soaked in ¼ cup water
¼ cup unsweetened applesauce
Vegetable cooking spray

STEPS IN PREPARATION:
1. Cream margarine in a medium bowl. Add brown sugar substitute and egg, and beat well.
2. Sift together flour, baking powder, and spice; add to creamed mixture, beating well. Stir in raisins and applesauce.
3. Spread mixture in an 8-inch square baking pan coated with cooking spray, and bake at 350° for 25 minutes. Let cool. Cut into 24 bars.

DATE-OAT BARS
Yield: 2 dozen bars

EACH SERVING **Amount:** 1 bar		
Exchanges: 1 Starch ½ Fat **Chol:** Tr.	**Calories:** 80 **Carbo:** 13 gm **Protein:** 1 gm	**Fat:** 3 gm **Fiber:** Tr. **Sodium:** 111 mg

INGREDIENTS:

1 (8-ounce) package pitted dates, chopped
1 tablespoon all-purpose flour
½ cup water
¾ cup unsweetened grated coconut

½ cup reduced-calorie margarine
Sugar substitute to equal ⅓ cup sugar
2½ cups uncooked quick-cooking oats
½ teaspoon vanilla extract
Vegetable cooking spray

STEPS IN PREPARATION:

1. Combine chopped dates and flour in a large mixing bowl. Toss lightly to coat.
2. Place water in a 1-cup glass measure; microwave at HIGH for 2 to 3 minutes or until boiling. Pour water over dates.
3. Add coconut, margarine, and sugar substitute to date mixture, stirring well. Microwave at HIGH for 2 to 3 minutes or until thickened, stirring at 1-minute intervals.
4. Add oats and vanilla to date mixture, mixing well.
5. Spoon mixture into a 9-inch square baking pan coated with cooking spray; press evenly into bottom of pan. Cover and refrigerate until set.
6. Cut into 24 bars, and store in an airtight container in refrigerator.

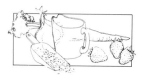

Appendix

Glossary

CALORIE - a unit of heat that measures the amount of energy in food.

CARBOHYDRATE - a major nutrient found in sugars, breads, cereals, vegetables, fruit, and milk; provides 4 calories per gram weight.

CHOLESTEROL - a fat-like substance which is made in the liver and found in animal foods.

DIABETES MELLITUS - failure of body cells to utilize carbohydrates because of inadequate production or use of insulin.

DIETETIC FOODS - foods prepared for special diets, such as low-fat, low-sodium, sugar-free, calorie-reduced, low-cholesterol—not all are suitable for diabetics.

DIGESTION - the breakdown of foods in the digestive tract into simple substances the body can use for energy and nourishment.

ENRICHED FOODS - foods made from refined grains to which one or more nutrients have been added to increase the nutrient value.

FAT - a major nutrient found in meats, eggs, milk and milk products, oils, margarine, salad dressings, and nuts which provides 9 calories per gram weight.

FIBER - that part of food which is not digested and adds bulk but no calories to the diet.

FOOD EXCHANGE - a group of foods which contain similar nutrients.

FREE FOODS - foods which have few calories and carbohydrates and do not need to be counted as Exchanges.

GLUCOSE - a simple sugar found in the blood which is made either by the digestion of food or from other carbohydrate and protein sources found in the body.

GRAM - a unit of weight in the metric system; one ounce equals 28.25 grams.

GLYCEMIC INDEX - a method of predicting the effect that different carbohydrate containing foods have on one's blood sugar.

HYPERGLYCEMIA - high blood glucose (sugar) levels.

HYPOGLYCEMIA - low blood glucose (sugar) levels.

INSULIN - a hormone made by the pancreas which is needed by the body to use carbohydrates.

INSULIN REACTION - a rapid fall in the blood glucose level due to the action of injected insulin.

MEAL PLAN - a guide used to show the number of Exchanges to eat at each meal.

MINERALS - a group of nutrients necessary for life found in small amounts in foods.

MONOUNSATURATED FAT - a neutral fat which does not increase or decrease serum (blood) cholesterol levels.

NUTRIENT - a substance necessary for life and found in food.

NUTRITION - the process by which the body uses food to nourish cells.

POLYUNSATURATED FAT - a fat found in plants which tends to lower serum (blood) cholesterol levels.

PROTEIN - a major nutrient which is essential for life and needed for building and repairing body cells and which is found in meats, eggs, milk, and milk products. Proteins provide 4 calories per gram weight.

REGISTERED DIETITIAN - a professional educated in nutrition; recognized in the health field as the primary provider of nutrition care, education and counseling.

SATURATED FAT - a fat which tends to raise serum (blood) cholesterol level and is usually found as solid fat.

STARCH - a complex form of carbohydrate which is changed to sugar during digestion.

TRYGLYCERIDES - a fat normally present in the blood, made from food which may be affected by excess weight, a high fat diet, alcohol, and sugar.

VITAMIN - a nutrient necessary for life found in small amounts in foods.

Table of Equivalents for Sugar Substitutes

BRAND NAME	SUBSTITUTION FOR SUGAR	BRAND NAME	SUBSTITUTION FOR SUGAR
Adolph's (powder)		**Sucaryl (liquid)**	
2 shakes of jar	= 1 rounded teaspoon sugar	⅛ teaspoon	= 1 teaspoon sugar
¼ teaspoon	= 1 tablespoon sugar	⅓ teaspoon	= 1 tablespoon sugar
1 teaspoon	= ¼ cup sugar	½ teaspoon	= 4 teaspoons sugar
2½ teaspoons	= ⅔ cup sugar	1½ teaspoons	= ¼ cup sugar
1 tablespoon	= ¾ cup sugar	1 tablespoon	= ½ cup sugar
4 teaspoons	= 1 cup sugar		
		Superose (liquid)	
		4 drops	= 1 teaspoon sugar
		⅛ teaspoon	= 2 teaspoons sugar
Equal (powder)*		⅛ teaspoon plus 4 drops	= 1 tablespoon sugar
1 packet	= 2 teaspoons sugar	1½ teaspoons	= ½ cup sugar
		1 tablespoon	= 1 cup sugar
Fasweet (liquid)		**Sugar Twin (powder)**	
⅛ teaspoon	= 1 teaspoon sugar	1 teaspoon	= 1 teaspoon sugar
¼ teaspoon	= 2 teaspoons sugar		
⅓ teaspoon	= 1 tablespoon sugar	**Sugar Twin, Brown (powder)**	
1 tablespoon	= ½ cup sugar	1 teaspoon	= 1 teaspoon brown sugar
2 tablespoons	= 1 cup sugar		

*Use only after cooking or in uncooked dishes.
Sugar equivalents for various brand names of sugar substitutes are listed for your convenience only and not as an endorsement.

Table of Equivalents for Sugar Substitutes

BRAND NAME	SUBSTITUTION FOR SUGAR	BRAND NAME	SUBSTITUTION FOR SUGAR
Sweet N' Low (powder)		**Sweet One (powder)**	
1/10 teaspoon	= 1 teaspoon sugar	1 packet	= 2 teaspoons sugar
1 packet	= 2 teaspoons sugar	3 packets	= ¼ cup sugar
⅓ teaspoon	= 1 tablespoon sugar	4 packets	= ⅓ cup sugar
1 teaspoon	= ¼ cup sugar	6 packets	= ½ cup sugar
1¼ teaspoons	= ⅓ cup sugar	12 packets	= 1 cup sugar
2 teaspoons	= ½ cup sugar		
4 teaspoons	= 1 cup sugar	**Sweet-10 (liquid)**	
		10 drops	= 1 teaspoon sugar
Sweet N' Low, Brown (powder)		½ teaspoon	= 4 teaspoons sugar
¼ teaspoon	= 1 tablespoon brown sugar	1½ teaspoons	= ¼ cup sugar
1 teaspoon	= ¼ cup brown sugar	1 tablespoon	= ½ cup sugar
1⅓ teaspoons	= ⅓ cup brown sugar	2 tablespoons	= 1 cup sugar
2 teaspoons	= ½ cup brown sugar		
4 teaspoons	= 1 cup brown sugar	**Zero-Cal (liquid)**	
		10 drops	= 1 teaspoon sugar
Sweet'ner (powder)		30 drops	= 1 tablespoon sugar
1 packet	= 2 teaspoons sugar	¾ teaspoon	= 2 tablespoons sugar
		1 tablespoon	= ½ cup sugar
Sweet Magic (powder)		2 tablespoons	= 1 cup sugar
1 packet	= 2 teaspoons sugar		

Sugar equivalents for various brand names of sugar substitutes are listed for your convenience only and not as an endorsement.

Spice and Herb Chart

SPICE OR HERB	MEATS, FISH, AND POULTRY	VEGETABLES AND PASTA	SALADS	EGGS AND CHEESE
Basil	Lamb, Pork, Liver, Veal, Fish Fillets, Shrimp, Tuna, Chicken, Venison, Duck, Turkey	Peas, Eggplant, Green Beans, Cauliflower, Squash, Tomatoes, Onions, Soups	Egg, Seafood, Tossed Green, Tomato, Chicken, Cucumber	Scrambled Eggs, Cheese Strata, Omelets, Cheese Sauce
Bay Leaves	Stews, Pot Roast, Tripe, Fish, Tongue, Corned Beef	Beets, Carrots, Stewed Tomatoes, Boiled Potatoes, Soups	Aspic, Fish	
Black Pepper	Steaks, Chops, Roast, Stews, Chicken, Game, Casseroles	Green Beans, Squash, Beets, Spinach, Peas	Tossed Green, Potato, Pickled Beets, Bean	
Caraway	Pork, Tripe, Liver, Lamb Stew, Beef Stew, Tongue	Potatoes, Sauerkraut, Carrots, Cabbage, Noodles, Asparagus	Cole Slaw, Beets, Green Bean, Cucumber	
Cloves	Baked Ham, Stews, Pot Roast, Spiced Tongue, Game Stews, Venison, Roast Chicken	Winter Squash, Onions, Tomatoes, Sweet Potatoes	Spiced Apple, Spiced Peach	
Dill Weed	Corned Beef, Beef Stew, Pork Stew, Pork Roast, Fish, Chicken, Game Stews	Noodles, New Potatoes, Green Vegetables, Cauliflower	Tossed Green, Green Beans, Cucumber, Potato, Pickled Beet, Cole Slaw, Tuna	Deviled Eggs, Creamed Eggs, Cottage Cheese, Scrambled Eggs, Omelets

Spice and Herb Chart

SPICE OR HERB	MEATS, FISH, AND POULTRY	VEGETABLES AND PASTA	SALADS	EGGS AND CHEESE
Marjoram	Veal, Stews, Beef, Fish, Pork, Venison, Rabbit, Chicken, Goose, Duck, Turkey	Carrots, Zucchini, Peas, Spinach, Soups, Onions	Tossed Green, Chicken, Seafood	Omelets, Scrambled Eggs, Soufflés
Oregano	Ground Beef, Pork, Lamb, Meat Loaf, Chicken, Guinea Hen, Shrimp, Lobster, Liver	Tomatoes, Cabbage, Lentils, Broccoli, Soups, Onions	Tomato Aspic, Fish, Cucumber, Bean, Potato	Soufflés, Omelets, Cheese Sauce, Scrambled Eggs
Paprika	Beef, Stew, Fish, Lobster, Chicken, Fish Chowder, Casseroles	Potato, Corn, Rice, Casseroles, Noodles	Potato, Macaroni, Chicken, Tuna	Deviled Eggs, Creamed Eggs, Cheese Sauce, Cheese Strata
Red Pepper	Stews, Italian Dishes, Chicken, Seafood Creole, Fish, Casseroles	Casseroles	Seafood, Chicken, Turkey	Cheese Strata, Cheese Sauce, Omelets
Rosemary	Pork, Veal, Poultry, Beef, Fish, Wild Fowl, Capon, Duck, Rabbit, Venison, Lamb	Peas, Spinach, Cauliflower, Turnips, Soups	Fruit, Tomato, Cucumber	Deviled Eggs, Scrambled Eggs, Soufflés

	Meats	Vegetables	Salads	Eggs & Cheese
Sage	Cottage Cheese, Stews, Pork, Lamb, Goose, Turkey, Rabbit, Fish, Chicken, Duck	Lima Beans, Eggplant, Onions, Tomatoes, Soups, Carrots	Tomato, Tossed Green, Bean	Cottage Cheese, Creamed Eggs, Soufflés
Savory	Turkey, Hamburger, Pork, Veal, Stews, Meat Loaf, Chicken, Rabbit, Fish Fillets, Shrimp	Beans, Rice, Lentils, Sauerkraut, Soups	Mixed Green, Bean, Tomato	Deviled Eggs, Scrambled Eggs, Omelets
Tarragon	Veal, Steaks, Chops, Chicken, Duck, Pheasant, Cornish Hens, Seafood, Lamb	Cauliflower, Beans, Lentils, Rice, Peas, Soups	Salmon, Tuna, Tossed Green, Bean, Chicken, Egg	Deviled Eggs, Cottage Cheese, Omelets
Thyme	Fish Fillets, Lamb, Beef, Meat Loaf, Stews, Liver, Chicken, Venison, Scallops, Turkey	Beets, Onions, Carrots, Brussel Sprouts, Zucchini, Asparagus	Pickled Beets, Tomato, Aspic, Cole Slaw, Chicken	Deviled Eggs, Soufflés, Omelets, Cottage Cheese
White Pepper	Stew, Veal, Fish, Casseroles	Cauliflower, Cabbage, Rice, Asparagus, Potatoes	Salmon, Tomato, Tuna, Shrimp, Chicken, Turkey	Deviled Eggs, Cheese Sauce, Creamed Eggs, Cheese Strata

Nutrient Chart

NUTRIENT	FUNCTIONS IN YOUR BODY	MAJOR FOOD SOURCES
Carbohydrates	Supply energy. Help body use other nutrients.	Cereals, fruits, vegetables, breads, sugars, milk, honey, cakes, cookies, pies, pasta.
Fats	Supply energy. Help maintain body temperature. Transport fat-soluble vitamins.	Margarine, butter, oils, shortening, cream, nuts, bacon, olives, whole milk.
Proteins	Build and repair body tissues. Help balance body chemicals. Supply energy.	Meat, poultry, fish, milk, cheese, nuts, dried peas and beans.
Vitamins		
Vitamin A	Helps eyes adjust to dim light. Helps keep skin healthy. Helps resist infection. Helps bones grow.	Liver, butter, cream, whole milk, egg yolk, broccoli, collards, spinach, carrots, sweet potatoes, pumpkin, winter squash, apricots, cantaloupe, greens.
Vitamin C	Helps hold body cells together. Helps heal wounds. Helps build bones and teeth. Helps absorb iron.	Oranges, grapefruit, cantaloupe, strawberries, raw cabbage, tomatoes, broccoli, green pepper.
Vitamin D	Helps body use calcium and phosphorous.	Liver, fortified milk, egg yolk (exposure to sunlight produces vitamin D in the skin).
Vitamin E	Helps keep red blood cells intact. Helps keep body fats intact.	Wheat germ, polyunsaturated vegetable oils.

Nutrient	Functions	Sources
Vitamin K	Is necessary for clotting blood.	Liver, spinach, greens, cabbage, cauliflower.
Thiamin (B1)	Helps body get energy from food. Helps keep nervous system healthy. Promotes good appetite and digestion.	Liver and other organ meats, meats, especially pork, poultry, whole-grain and enriched breads and cereals, nuts, dried peas and beans.
Riboflavin (B2)	Helps body get energy from food. Promotes healthy skin, eyes, and clear vision.	Milk, organ meats, egg white, enriched breads and cereals.
Niacin	Helps body produce energy. Aids digestion and good appetite. Helps keep skin, tongue, nervous system, and digestive tract healthy.	Lean meat, fish, poultry, liver, peanuts, whole-grain and enriched breads and cereals.
Cobalamine (B12)	Helps build red blood cells. Promotes healthy nervous system.	Liver and other organ meats, meat, fish, poultry.
Pyridoxine (B6)	Helps body use food. Helps build blood cells.	Egg yolk, whole-grain cereals, liver, peanuts, soybeans.
Minerals		
Calcium	Builds bones and teeth. Helps clot blood. Helps nerves, muscles, and heart to function well.	Milk, cheese, yogurt, buttermilk, tofu.
Phosphorous	Builds bones and teeth. Helps body get energy from food.	Milk and milk products, meat, fish, poultry, eggs, nuts, dried peas and beans.

Nutrient Chart

NUTRIENT	FUNCTIONS IN YOUR BODY	MAJOR FOOD SOURCES
Minerals		
Iron	Forms part of red blood cells. Helps body get energy from food.	Liver and other organ meats, egg yolk, meat, poultry, oysters, enriched and whole-grain breads and cereals, dried peas and beans.
Sodium	Helps control water balance. Regulates nerve impulses and muscle contractions.	Salt, meat, fish, poultry, milk and milk products, eggs.
Potassium	Helps control water balance. Regulates nerve impulses, muscle contractions, and heart rhythm.	Fruits, vegetables, meat, fish, poultry, milk and milk products.
Iodine	Regulates energy.	Seafood, iodized salt.
Magnesium	Is part of bones and teeth. Helps body use carbohydrates. Helps regulate nerve and muscle contractions.	Whole-grain cereals, nuts, dried peas and beans, milk, meat, leafy green vegetables.
Copper	Helps form red blood cells. Aids absorption and use of iron. Helps body get energy from food.	Liver, shellfish, meat, nuts, dried peas and beans, whole-grain cereals.
Water	Helps build and bathe body cells. Aids digestion and absorption. Helps lubricate joints and organs. Regulates body temperature.	All liquids such as water, coffee, tea, soft drinks, fruit and vegetable juices, milk, ice.

RECIPE INDEX

SUBJECT INDEX

Alcohol, 5
American Diabetes Association,
  2, 8, 10, 20
American Dietetic Association,
  The, 2, 8, 10, 20
American Heart Association, 2, 8
Amino acids, 3-4
Atherosclerosis, 6
Attitude, 8, 128
Brown bagging, 29-30
Calcium, 18
Calories, 27, 29, 45
  curbs, 67, 74, 104, 121, 132,
    149, 194, 199, 206
  exchange counts, 9, 10, 12, 15,
    16, 18, 19
  in free foods, 21
  in nutrients, 2-5
  on labels, 24
Carbohydrates, 6, 27
  exchange values, 9, 10, 15, 16,
    18, 22
  explanation, 2-3
  function, 1
  on labels, 24
  in sugar, 25
  in weight control, 137
Cardiovascular
  complications, 8
  disease, 7
Cholesterol, 3, 27
  dietary, 4-5
  elevated, 6, 7-8
  in meat, 13
Diabetes mellitus, 3
  diet plan for, 5, 6, 9, 27
  discussion of, 6-7
  during illness, 22-23
  exercise, 8
  gestational, 7
  meal plan for, 29
  Types, 6-7, 8
Dietary guidelines, 2-6, 7, 8, 23
Dietetic, 24

Dietetic scales, 27
Dining out, 28-29, 113, 169
Exchange lists, 5, 6, 8, 24
  explanation of, 9-10
  Fat, 19-20
  Fruit, 16-18
  Meat, 12-15
  Milk, 18-19
  Starch/Bread, 10-12
  Vegetable, 15-16
Exercise, 41, 48, 85, 92, 107, 116,
  128, 155, 172, 200
  discussion of, 8
Fast food, 29
Fats, 8
  calories in, 2
  daily need, 6
  defatting stock, 121
  exchange values, 9, 10, 12, 13,
    18, 19
  function, 1
  guidelines, 4
  in food preparation, 12, 27,
    38, 42, 58, 94, 98, 138, 149,
    184
  in foods, 18, 29, 35, 114
  on labels, 24
  list, 9, 19-20
  monounsaturated, 4
  polyunsaturated, 4
  saturated, 4-5, 13, 19, 104
Fatty acids, 4
Fiber
  explanation of, 3
  function, 1
  guidelines for, 2
  in fruit, 16
  in meat, 13
  in vegetables, 15
  in whole grains, 10, 43
Fish
  oils, 110, 114
  preparation of, 94
Free foods, 21